Individualism and

BIG BUSINESS

Since humans are the most intelligent and also the most easily taught of animals, one would expect them to be the most highly individuated. No two persons are exactly alike in their physical and mental potentialities, and certainly no two individuals, even identical twins reared in the same family, have the same experiences. Human beings are thus potentially less alike than the individuals of any other species. It is most surprising therefore, that they have chosen to live in closely organized groups whose members carry on a variety of specialized activities but are mutually interdependent for the satisfaction of practically all their fundamental needs. Many other mammalian species live in herds or packs, but the organization in these is minimal. The only division of activities is that devolving upon the two sexes by their different roles in connection with reproduction, while social control is a simple matter of the poorer fighters giving precedence to the better ones. To find anything which even remotely resembles the complexity of human societies, one must go to the social insects, such as the ants and bees. Here the cooperation which is necessary for the survival of the community is assured by the physical specialization of the various groups of workers, fighters, and so forth, and by a high development of instincts. Since humans lack such instincts, it becomes necessary to subject them to an extraordinarily long and elaborate training if they are to function successfully as members of a society. We are, in fact, anthropoid apes trying to live like termites, and, as any philosophical observer can attest, not doing too well at it.[*]

[*] Ralph Linton, *The Tree of Culture,*
Alfred A. Knopf, Inc., New York, 1957, p. 11.

Individualism and
BIG BUSINESS

LEONARD R. SAYLES

Professor
Graduate School of Business
Columbia University

**McGRAW-HILL
BOOK COMPANY, INC.**

New York
San Francisco
Toronto
London

CONTRIBUTORS AND
THEIR AFFILIATIONS

Ivar Berg
Associate Professor, Graduate School of Business, Columbia University

Wilfred Brown
Chairman, Glacier Metal Company, Ltd.

Margaret Chandler
Professor of Sociology, University of Illinois

Eliot Chapple
President, E. D. Chapple Company and Principal Research Scientist,
Rockland State Hospital

Harlan Cleveland
Assistant Secretary of State for International Organizations

Eli Ginzberg
Professor, Graduate School of Business, Columbia University

Lawrence Hinkle, Jr.
Internist, New York Hospital-Cornell Medical Center

Margaret Mead
Associate Curator of Ethnology, American Museum of Natural History

Wilbert Moore
Professor, Princeton University

George Strauss
Professor, School of Business Administration,
University of California at Berkeley

Ross Webber
Graduate student, Ph.D. Candidate, Graduate School of Business,
Columbia University

William F. Whyte
Professor, New York State School of Industrial and Labor Relations,
Cornell University

Foreword

Over extended periods of time, the institutions that earn acceptance and thrive in any society are those that provide personal satisfactions for the individuals within the orbit of their influence. Opportunity to express oneself is a basic urge, but the manner and the institutions within which self-expression occur differ from person to person. The ultimate destiny of the business corporation, now so pervasive and influential in contemporary life, may be determined more by its effect upon those directly and indirectly associated in its activities than by its capacity to provide material abundance or by competitive political ideologies.

Organizations are conditioned by the extent to which their participants are able and willing to exercise initiative and imaginative action within the framework of predetermined purposes and policies. On the one hand, initiative exercised to frustrate the corporate purpose can undermine the group effectiveness. On the other, the dead hand of excessive conformity and routinized behavior, particularly in the echelons of management, subtly saps the vitality of an organization and impair its efficiency.

A business corporation will achieve its full opportunities for service to mankind only if it finds ways to maximize the incentives for initiative and prudent risk taking among its members. Yet continuous pressure to achieve harmonious integration with other individuals at all levels, the psychologists tell us, is the certain path to lack of creativity, imagination, and spontaneity.

The extent to which the nature and structure of a large organization provide opportunities and inducements for self-expression, the degree of awareness in business organizations of the importance of encouraging individuality, and the insights that might be provided by the behavioral sciences for understanding this most difficult problem, are subjects that have long interested the Graduate Faculty of Business of Columbia.

Under the direction of Professor Leonard Sayles and with the encouragement of financial sponsorship by the Louis B. Wolfson Foundation, a competent group of scholars and business leaders was assembled some months ago for an Arden House conference to discuss these matters. All agreed that the occasion was significantly instructive and deserved wider attention than was possible within a group of moderate size. Professor Sayles has skillfully annotated the basic presentations of the conference with extracts from the ensuing discussions and with his own rich scholarship and that of his colleagues in research.

Courtney C. Brown

Dean, Graduate School of Business
Columbia University

Preface

Some months ago the industrial relations faculty of the Graduate School of Business at Columbia was privileged to prepare a symposium reviewing some of our current research for a group of top executives of American corporations. On that occasion we were joined by several colleagues with whom we had had close contacts over the years. By means of both background papers and discussion we explored a series of problems of growing concern involving the relationship of individuals to large organizations. Our society is characteristically concerned with the opportunities for individual development in the economic as well as the social and political spheres of American life.

I have now had the opportunity to review our efforts and have endeavored to identify the common themes and conclusions. The original material was contributed by Professors Berg, Ginzberg, and myself of the Columbia faculty and Professors Moore of Princeton and Whyte and Hinkle of Cornell—all of whom participated in this program.

We are also most fortunate in being able to republish an essay by Assistant Secretary of State Harlan Cleveland. He had been invited to attend our original program, but the press of business had prevented his appearance. We are pleased to have him represented through this medium.

With these materials as the core, I have endeavored to build a view of the large organization based on the sophisticated research and insights of a number of other observers. The greater part of the material has not heretofore been published, but I have drawn on several published articles where the ideas were germane to our major themes.

I can probably be accused of "loading the dice." This volume has brought together the views of a number of highly expert observers of the modern organization who, for the most part, do not share the commonly accepted view that it is inimical to the welfare of the individual participant. While they realize that many problems remain unsolved, they feel that a realistic conception of the processes of organization provides the best basis for dealing with them.

Unfortunately, a large number of social scientists and journalists
(and often the distinction between the two is not clear) have not taken
the trouble to look inside the institutions they see in such damning
terms. They carry over their prejudices about mass society to a general,
undifferentiated view of the large organization. Unfortunately, or
really fortunately, reality is not so simple as their diagnoses, nor is
the world of large-scale organizations so sick as they would have us
believe.

I have found another satisfaction in editing these materials, aside
from the chance to show the other side of the coin. I have had the
privilege of working in one capacity or another with most of the contributors during recent years and have gained immeasurably from the
association. It is with pleasure that I have endeavored to show the
common threads in the analytical findings of these social scientists,
physicians, and administrators.

Leonard R. Sayles

Contents

chapter 1

Introduction: stating the problem

We usually assume, with some reason, that people living in every age believe they understand their lives and times. Only the historian discovers that in the past they have had little conception of the intrinsic characteristics of their institutions, or of the distinctive ways they made their living, raised families, engaged in social intercourse, and built philosophical systems. Today widespread education and mass communication media have so increased our own level of confidence that we do really believe that we comprehend the world about us. Only on rare occasions is this sophistication shattered. A good recent example of a devastating criticism is the theory of two cultures advanced by an eminent British essayist and novelist.

C. P. Snow has gained the ear of most of the reading Western world with his charge that two of the most important groups in our society have almost no conception of each other's point of view and life. Many readers will recognize the chasm that he claims separates the natural scientist and engineer from the literary, humanist intellectual.

But less well publicized is Snow's observation, shared by many who are represented in this volume, that this polarization is but another example of the failure of "traditional culture" to take much interest, except for occasional condemnation, in the industrial revolution and the technology and organizations it spawned.[1]

[1] C. P. Snow, *The Two Cultures and the Scientific Revolution,* Cambridge University Press, New York, 1959, p. 24.

1

Snow is largely speaking of the past when he says, "Almost none of the talent, almost none of the imaginative energy, went back into the revolution which was producing the wealth," but he is speaking of the present when he remarks on the lag in the intelligent interest shown by applied social science and the literary world in the world of business, once one gets past a few worn stereotypes about assembly lines, union leaders, and good and bad bosses.

Snow is aware of this gap as he comments:

> How many educated people know anything about productive industry, old-style or new? . . . Buttons aren't very complicated things. . . . Yet I would bet that out of men getting firsts in arts subjects at Cambridge this year, not one in ten could give the loosest analysis of the human organization which it [industry] needs. . . .
>
> In the United States, perhaps, there is a wider nodding acquaintance with industry, but . . . no American novelist of any class has ever been able to assume that his audience had it. He can assume, and only too often does, an acquaintance with a pseudofeudal society like the . . . Old South —but not with industrial society.
>
> Yet the personal relations in a productive organization are of the greatest subtlety and interest. They are very deceptive. They look as though they ought to be the personal relations that one gets in any hierarchical structure with a chain of command, like a division in the army. . . . In practice they are much more complex than that, and anyone used to the straight chain of command gets lost the instant he sets foot in an industrial organization. No one in any country, incidentally, knows yet what these personal relations ought to be.[2]

To be sure, particularly in this country but also in Western Europe, a number of careful studies and commentaries on the world of work have been made. But they have not been studies of the organizations produced by the industrial revolution. With few exceptions, business as it involves organizations, large aggregations of people who work in various relationships one to another, much more complicated than those symbolized by the old words "boss" and "employee," has been largely untouched by the serious writer of social science or fiction.

One of our most prominent social scientists in the United States has recently observed that the members of his profession have consciously avoided studying the world of business, particularly the realm

[2] *Ibid.,* pp. 32–33.

of management itself.[3] The preference has been for studies of less-privileged or problem groups such as racial minorities, criminals, hourly workers, prostitutes, and the mentally ill. In fact serious intra-faculty disputes at a major business school have been attributed to the fact that while teaching stresses a top-management point of view, research at the institution has concentrated on immediate production problems and the hourly employee. Of course, the reluctance of the social scientists to move into centers of power and prestige has been more than matched by the reluctance of management to encourage research at its own level as distinct from studies of employee morale or consumer motivations.

While little systematic research has been conducted on the actual nature of organizations, particularly beyond the level of clerks or machine operators, an increasing flow of condemnatory tracts and strong indictments of the modern large organization, particularly but not exclusively the business organization, has come from the press. Here is but a small sampling of some of their conclusions:

The formal organization, directive leadership, and management controls tend to create a situation in which the employees adapt by behaving in ways antagonistic to the desires of management. Management, in turn, tends to react in a way that increases the antagonism, which in turn leads to a barrier toward upward communication of these antagonistic activities by the employees who are aware of and centered toward management's needs. As a result there begins to exist a feeling of two worlds; the employee and the management. . . .[4]

An analysis of the basic properties of relatively mature human beings and formal organization leads to the conclusion that there is an inherent incongruency between the self-actualization of the two. This basic incongruency creates a situation of conflict, frustration, and failure for the participants. . . .[5]

In a world dominated by a vast system of abstractions, managers may become cold with principle and do what local and immediate masters of

[3] Prof. Paul Lazarsfeld, "New Developments in Social Science for Business," unpublished lecture before the seminar, Williams College, Aug. 14, 1962.
[4] Chris Argyris, *Personality and Organization: The Conflict between the System and the Individual,* Harper & Row, Publishers, Incorporated, New York, 1957, p. 163.
[5] *Ibid.,* p. 175.

men could never do. Their social insulation results in deadened feelings in the face of the impoverishment of life in the lower orders and its stultification in the upper circles. We do not mean merely that there are managers of bureaucracies and of communication agencies who scheme (although, in fact, there are, and their explicit ideology is one of manipulation); but more, we mean that the social control of the system is such that irresponsibility is organized into it.

Organized irresponsibility, in this impersonal sense, is a leading characteristic of modern industrial societies everywhere. On every hand the individual is confronted with seemingly remote organizations; he feels dwarfed and helpless before the managerial cadres and their manipulated and manipulative minions.[6]

Secondly, the rise in the scale of organizations raises serious questions for the freedom and dignity of the person. The price that we pay for organization is hierarchy, and even though the force of disloyalty and insubordination (without which, of course, progress would probably be impossible) acts as an important check on the growth of hierarchy, the fact remains that the removal of other barriers to large scale organization means that a larger and larger proportion of people are going to have to live their lives as subordinate members of a hierarchy. The problem of the defense of the individual against his hierarchical superiors therefore becomes more and more acute.[7]

There is nothing novel about teaching people how to manipulate other people, and GE's scientific psychological techniques bear a strong resemblance to the how-to-be-a-success precepts standard in the United States for decades. What is different about them is their justification. They are not presented on the grounds that they will help make people do what you want them to do so that you can make more money. GE trainees see it in much more eleemosynary terms. They do like the part about selling yourself to others so you can get ahead, for they think a lot about this. But they don't abide the thought of enemies on the other side of the counter; they see the manipulative skills as something that in the long run will make other people *happy*. When, in years to come, the trainees are charged with the destiny of subordinates—a possibility most take remarkably much for granted—they will be able to achieve a stable, well-adjusted work group. They won't drive subordinates, they explain. They will motivate them.[8]

[6] C. Wright Mills, *White Collar*, Oxford University Press, New York, 1951, p. 111.
[7] Kenneth Boulding, "The Jungle of Hugeness," *Saturday Review*, Mar. 1, 1958, p. 50.
[8] William H. Whyte, Jr., *The Organization Man*, Simon and Schuster, Inc., New York, 1956.

I have been talking of the extension of the team to a field where it does not belong. Even in fields where the group is vital, however, the current emphasis on the team is having some equally inhibiting effects. Just as it has obscured the role of the individual in creation and discovery in such activities as research and communication, so in the regular work of running an organization it is obscuring the function of leadership.

Such emphasis is particularly unnecessary at this time because the whole tendency of modern organization life is to muffle the importance of individual leadership. . . .[9]

While differing in their emphases, the authors of these indictments come to mutually complementary conclusions concerning the debilitating effects of the large organization on the individual, his initiative, and his rights to self-determination and self-fulfillment.

These social critics would probably agree on the following as a first approximation of the sources of human problems in the large organization:

■ Its very size: Individualism cannot flourish where masses of people are brought together in a common endeavor; only some highly abstract version of the individual can be dealt with by the organization.

■ Its emphasis on hierarchy and extreme specialization; the power of the boss to dominate and the fear of incurring his displeasure and of violating the rigid rules, narrow job boundaries, and standard procedures.

■ Its emphasis on loyalty, on total commitment of the individual to the organization and the efforts to encourage such loyalty at the expense of identifications with other institutions in society such as trade unions or alternative sources of employment.

■ Its use of techniques to hold the individual tightly, such as seniority benefits, pension plans, and "manipulative supervision," which discourage rebelliousness and urge rote conformity.

■ Its efforts to exclude "strong" individuals or people who differ from some modal patterns and who might be disruptive to a docile human environment.

All these elements fit together and have a certain amount of face validity, as the social scientist would say. All of us have experienced or heard about elements that seem to confirm these strong accusations. But the crucial question is whether systematic inquiry would disclose the same pattern.

Several of us on the faculty of the Graduate School of Business at

[9] *Ibid.*, p. 53.

Columbia became interested, five years ago, in the problems of comprehending the large business organization as a human system. Although four monographs have been completed which deal with parts of the total, we could hardly claim to have conducted definitive research. Some months ago, however, we had the opportunity to exchange our views and findings with colleagues from business and other universities in an Arden House Conference sponsored by the Wolfson Foundation. On reviewing the proceedings of this conference and the papers that were prepared, we concluded that we could make some contribution toward correcting many of the oversimplifications and extreme positions represented by the indictments cited above. The present volume is an effort to bring together these materials from lectures, monographs, research, and discussion as they apply to the question of the impact of the large business organization on individual initiative.

It would be unfair to imply that the question is solely or even primarily a matter of academic interest. The large business organization is not only one of the newest institutions in our society; it is also one of the most vital. Few would dispute the fact that it occupies a position of great power. Is this power consistent with the requirements of a democratic, pluralistic society? Is the large organization obtaining a position of hegemony contrary to our social and political traditions? A parallel economic question is the challenge to the assumption that one gets greater efficiency with size. May there not be diminishing returns with "excessive" size, as represented by the problems of red tape, breakdowns in communication and leadership, and the like?

While the general public, like the academic man, is naturally and justifiably suspicious of concentrations of power, there are also rising expectations of what business should provide. Business not only must meet the economists' criteria of efficiency, but ought to provide satisfactions in the jobs it creates: not just economic satisfactions but social and psychological returns as well. These rising levels of expectation are hallmarks of our age of affluence, where purely physical returns are not enough.

And the businessman himself is beginning to ask questions. While a few years ago he might have been content to gain a degree of orderliness, of discipline, and of union-management harmony, he is now concerned with less tangible elements like motivation and creativity. In part, his concern reflects the changing balance in the labor force, which includes more white-collar, professional, and semiprofessional jobs where the individual is not tied to the machine and where there is a great leeway for individual contribution and judgment. It also represents the beginnings of a recognition that managerial work is as problematic and worthy of systematic behavioral analysis as is production work. Given the potentialities for success or failure in choices made and wisdom expended, these managerial jobs are probably even more worthy of attention.

Thus the present volume represents an effort to close the gap between the field of applied science, of systematic investigation and analysis (management and engineering), and the intellectual world, although it is admittedly an effort rather than a completed task. A parallel objective has been to highlight the need for systematic inquiry to replace highly speculative, oversimplified, unverified generalization. Each age has its explanation of man's failure to attain perfectibility. This is an age of urban living, of mass communication and culture, and of the large organization. All three are often indicted as a conspiracy to thwart the individual in attaining his destiny.

Few would have the temerity to deny the existence of major social problems. But sweeping indictment makes little contribution, in the field of social science at least. Few expect large organizations to disappear. Our need is for more dispassionate investigation. We hope the data and the themes presented in the chapters to follow will encourage such inquiry; surely in our age few fields of investigation are more challenging.

Perhaps we should warn the prospective reader that the general conclusions reached in this volume present a picture of the large organization and its problem of reconciling individual initiative with institutional needs far different from that usually offered the public. We shall find, in fact, that these organizations bear little resemblance to the stereotypes of the most vehement critics. Bigness poses many persisting problems; but they are not the ones usually cited, nor are the potentially fruitful solutions those most popular today. Thus Snow's indictment stands: too many prescriptions for nonexistent ailments, based on the failure to stop and look at what actually occurs in large organizations, and, concomitantly, too little attention to the real problems surrounding effective use of people in complex structures.

In Parts I and II we shall try to compare what is known about life in large organizations and their employees with the myths that have arisen. Part III examines the problems that are not myths; for some, solutions are presented; others remain as future challenges.

PART I

*What are large
organizations like?*

chapter 2

Dinosaurs and personal freedom*

It has become the fashion in recent years to cry havoc about one particular evidence of social complexity—the weedlike growth of large-scale bureaucracies, public and private. It is true, of course, that a finer division of labor and the availability of economies of scale encourage the erection of unwieldy-looking pyramids of authority. It is true that governments get bigger, business firms and labor unions get bigger, newspapers become fewer, and huge organizations make a growing proportion of the decisions that affect the welfare and destiny of us all. But is it true, as much of the current literature would imply, that this trend puts our welfare and destiny in fewer and fewer hands? Does the individual have less choice or more?

My impression is that "large-scale" organization generally implies loose organization. Precisely because big organizations make most of the vital decisions affecting our destiny, more people are participating in those decisions than ever before. The number of decisions that *are* important to our individual lives is multiplying so rapidly that it takes a growing proportion of the nation's available leadership to get them made at all. The result of bigness is actually a diffusion of the decision-making and decision-influencing process far beyond the wildest dreams of those worshipers at the shrine of Louis Brandeis, who wanted to keep power diffused by keeping the units of society small.

* This chapter is from the article by Harlan Cleveland, "Dinosaurs and Personal Freedom," which appeared in *Saturday Review*, Feb. 28, 1959, pp. 12–14, 36–37. Used by permission of the author and the *Saturday Review*.

In turn, the diffusion of power in such an interdependent society as ours means that each individual leader has more responsibility to his fellowmen than ever before. And so, as though in recompense for this added burden, the American executive leader finds he can exercise more freedom of choice than ever before—if he only learns how to operate within a large organization.

THE CASE FOR THE BRONTOSAURUS

In an article titled "The Jungle of Hugeness" in the *Saturday Review* in 1958, Kenneth Boulding argues that things look bad for the individual in a world dominated by huge organizations, but cheerfully concludes that there is a good deal of room in the interstices *between* the behemoths, where "individualists . . . and people who positively like smallness of scale" can nevertheless survive. In the "Great Forest of society," the brontosaurus can do a lot of harm if he steps on you, but his feet don't take up much of the available acreage and there is plenty left over for the nimble and quick.

Everybody looks at the world through his own knothole; but Mr. Boulding and I must be examining different worlds. Throughout this article he seems to assume that large organizations are single units, hierarchical, monolithic, and forbidding; that the only position of power in an organization is the number one spot; and that the interstices of freedom in our society are *outside* the large organizations. None of these propositions seems to me to have merit.

Mr. Boulding's alarm stems from the observation that what he calls the Organizational Revolution is tending

. . . toward ever greater degrees of hugeness. The electronic calculator, the punched card, operations research, and decision theory all point to a still further revolution in the making, to a still further removal of the scale barrier to the point, say, where General Motors (or the Pentagon, if by that time there is any distinction between the two) might absorb the *whole* American economy, and we would have, of course, a Communist State.

The case for capitalism is the case for smallness of scale; the case for Communism is the case against the Brontosaurus—that beyond a certain point, increase in the scale of organization results in a breakdown of communication, in a lack of flexibility, in bureaucratic stagnation and insensitivity. There is a great deal of evidence to show that with present techniques of organization the scale barrier is reached long before we get to an organization the size of Soviet Russia, and that an attempt to organize a large economy as a one-firm state is doomed to inefficiency, corruption, and cruelty.

At first sight, even in America, things look bad for the individual. . . .

Mr. Boulding is an economist, so I will have to assume that he has some evidence, not visible to my naked eyes, which persuades him that the successes of American capitalism are due to smallness of scale. But his general picture depends for its logic on an even stranger notion: that the only countervailing power that might affect, say, General Motors is power outside the General Motors Corporation. On the contrary, it is observable that very large organizations do not operate as single units with one commander in charge. Most of the checks and balances are internal to the system. The tensions within the system are many and so, therefore, are the opportunities for leadership.

In a household managed by people who can walk and talk, a baby begins to experience a sense of personal freedom when it masters the techniques of walking and talking. Just so, in a world dominated by large-scaleness, it is those individuals who learn to work with and in large-scale organizations who will have a rational basis for feeling free. There are, of course, plenty of free men who work for giant corporations or government agencies—but they aren't those who are so afraid of them that they scurry into the "interstices" of smallness. I have no doubt that a large number of middle-grade bureaucrats in the Soviet Union have so mastered the System that they are, in a sense, experiencing within its limits a significant measure of personal freedom. The reason is that the Soviet is not, as Mr. Boulding protests, a "one-firm state," but a myriad collection of organizations of manageable size bound together by leadership and a sense of destiny in ways not so fundamentally different from other nations as they (and we) like to assume.

Organizations *do* get bigger all the time. The Defense Department, whose growth so alarms Mr. Boulding, already employs 1,175,915 civilians (not to speak of soldiers, sailors, airmen and Marines) and uses nearly 10 per cent of our gross national product. It spends more than the whole national product of Canada, Japan, India, or Communist China, more than all states and local governments in the United States, including all public education for 40,000,000 people from kindergarten to state universities. As my colleague Jay Westcott puts it,

Every other American institution or business is a dwarf by comparison with the Department of Defense. Defense assets are greater than the combined wealth of the 100 largest corporations in America. (Indeed, some of their wealth depends largely on their ability to get contracts from the Defense Department.) Some individual defense installations have a greater worth than does the Ford Motor Company. The annual purchases of the Air Force alone are larger in volume than the output of America's greatest industrial producer—General Motors. The array of items purchased, distributed, and used for defense is forty times as numerous as those marketed by Sears Roebuck and Company.

Do these facts mean the Defense Department is a dangerously monolithic organization, that there is no freedom in its military and civilian ranks, no interstices for individualists in the Pentagon building? The President of the United States has had difficulties trying to organize that Department's several satrapies under the more effective control of the Secretary of Defense. The Defense Department has never been a unit. The larger it gets, the less likely it is to achieve effective unity. If it did achieve the monolithic quality Mr. Boulding seems to fear, it would be dead on its feet. It is the internal administrative tensions in a bureaucracy which keep it alive. In this respect at least, a body politic is like the nervous system of an animal.

CONDITIONS OF SURVIVAL

"The bigger the organization," says Mr. Boulding, "the smaller the proportion of its members who can really be at the top of the hierarchy and participate in the major decisions, and the larger the proportion who must carry out policies which are set higher up." It is not clear to me that this is the nature of large-scale organization. I would be more inclined to argue that a large and powerful organization has so many more important decisions to be made that there is proportionately more, not less, decision-making authority to go around. The larger the organization and the wider its reach, the more lateral contacts it has to make and maintain, the more complexities must be sorted out by experts on complexity—which is to say leaders.

Moreover, in our society the larger the organization the more likely it is to be either a public agency or a private enterprise affected with the public interest. In such an organization the number of "major decisions" about *internal* management may simply rise in arithmetic ratio to size, but the decisions about *external* relationships, the consent-building decisions that are in the broadest sense of the term "political," surely rise in geometric ratio. It is observable that in a large organization affected with the public interest (a category which includes nearly all large business corporations and labor unions in our increasingly "mixed" economy), the nearer you get to the top of the hierarchy the fewer unreviewed decisions you make. The man who buys writing pads and pencils for a government agency is virtually his own boss, but the President of the United States has to operate in a world peopled with countervailing organizations in and out of government which believe his every move is of concern to them, and must therefore be cleared with them. The more countervailing organizations have to be consulted, the more members of the internal staff must be assigned to deal with them—and must therefore "participate in major decisions."

Finally, it is not true that in bigger organizations there is less room at the top. It may be that there is so little interesting "policy" to be made in some of the private corporations Mr. Boulding has studied that there is room for only one or two men to have the feeling they are "participating in major decisions." But a governmental agency wields such power that the lowliest field representative may legitimately feel that he is involved in major decisions. A junior field inspector of material for the Air Force may never participate in a "policy" conference with the Secretary of Defense, but his influence is great within his own sphere—and people judge themselves and are judged by others according to their influence (and their freedom of movement) within their own sphere. Doubtless, the local Communist Party hack in the U.S.S.R., even if he never sits in on a meeting of the Presidium, has an equally solid basis for high morale; he fixes his attention on the respects in which he is a big frog in a little pond, and chooses not to dwell on those aspects of his personal situation that would make him seem a tiny frog in the ocean of Soviet Communism. In spite of his unimpressive position on the totem pole of our agricultural bureaucracy, the county agricultural extension agent is a big man in his circle, disposing of substantial resources and representing, in the individual farmer's eyes, the power and weight of the U.S. Government.

I have known field missions of the U.S. foreign aid program in which virtually every employee had a vivid sense of importance or "participation in major decisions," because the enterprise itself was palpably important and the daily work of each person obviously set precedents and could establish (or wreck) diplomatic relationships with a foreign power.

Mr. Boulding concludes that "small organizations, even down to the level of the 'independent person' will survive in the interstices between large-scale organizations." In our interdependent society one does not easily find the referent for the term "independent person"; but I suspect that those individuals will *feel* independent and self-confident who have learned how to survive and grow *within* large-scale organizations, not how to escape into the interstices *between* them. Perhaps Mr. Boulding should have carried his image of the brontosaurus one step further: If my son (our family's specialist on dinosaurs) is correctly informed, these huge beasts were remarkable, like the elephant, for their surprisingly soft tread.

ADMINISTRATORS ALL

It is a measure of the national mood that at the peak of American power we should be seized with the worry that large-scale organization is somehow a Bad Thing—that the very administrative skill which enabled us to build this strength and brought us free-world leadership is itself a threat to freedom.

My thesis here is the reverse: It is precisely by the development of his administrative skills that Man preserves and extends his freedom. The complexity of modern society and the omnipresence of large-scale organizations not only provide an opportunity for the fullest development of the responsible self; they actually place a premium on the exercise of a greater measure of personal responsibility by more people than ever before.

One of the results of modern technology and organization, for example, is to reduce the margins for error in a thousand ways. A hundred years ago most of the inhabitants of this continent were scattered about on farms or in rural towns with plenty of room to spare. But now that two-thirds of us live in urban areas, our accountability to each other is greatly enhanced. Childhood activities which used to be tolerated in rural societies are now regarded in cities as "deviant behavior"; one suspects it is not high-spirited youth that has changed, but the norms of delinquency against which juvenile conduct is measured. Similarly, for adults, driving a Buick on a crowded speedway requires more continuous exercise of a sense of responsibility to others than driving a Model T on a rural byway. A pilot of an air transport has to make more split-second decisions, and is responsible for more lives, than the man who drove the stagecoach.

All this makes life more dangerous, both for the decision maker and for the rest of us who depend on his being right the first time. But do not these accretions of personal responsibility tend to increase the individual's sense of personal freedom?

Perhaps the most dramatic contemporary example is that of an air-defense team watching for enemy invasions through the Distant Early Warning line. As warning of attack becomes a matter of hours (and in the future even of minutes), a heavy responsibility to all of us rests on the young men who will interpret the electronic smears on their radar screens. Unleashing our capacity for massive retaliation against an enemy is a fearful responsibility; yet the demands of technology have not concentrated this decision but diffused it to the far corners of the earth where a sleepy GI could cost us precious time—or an overzealous one cost us much more than that.

In many less stirring but equally relevant ways, the complexity of society makes us all vulnerable to irresponsible action by others. If a man wanted to shoot up his neighbor in the Kentucky mountains, the other residents could avoid participation in the feud, which might smolder for generations as a "limited war" between two families. But a similar feud will not be tolerated by urban society. The interrelatedness of everything puts society's balance of power in the hands of the innocent bystander.

This increase in the extent to which each individual is personally responsible to others is most noticeable in a large bureaucracy. No one person "decides" anything; each "decision" of any importance is the product of an intricate process of brokerage involving individuals inside and outside the organization who feel some reason to be affected by the decision, or who have special knowledge to contribute to it. The more varied the organization's constituency, the more outside "veto-groups" will need to be taken into account. But even if no outside consultations were involved, sheer size would produce a complex process of decision. For a large organization is a deliberately created system of tensions into which each individual is expected to bring work-ways, viewpoints, and outside relationships markedly different from those of his colleagues. It is the administrator's task to draw from these disparate forces the elements of wise action from day to day, consistent with the purposes of the organization as a whole.

Such a bureaucratic tension system places a high premium on imagination, vigor, and qualities of personal leadership at all levels. The larger and more complex the organization, the more necessary it is for more of its members to learn and practice the art of building consent around a personal conviction—and reconciling it with the personal convictions of others. The finer the division of labor required, the more important it is for the scientist or economist or other specialist to understand the process by which his expert judgments are stirred into the administrative stew.

The expert is no longer just responsible for "presenting all the alternatives" in a careful, scientific, and scholarly manner. He must also figure out who to present them to, and how, and what he wants to see happen after one of his "alternatives" is accepted. The expert is also responsible, in short, for being not only right but effective: for getting his thinking understood by non-specialists, and for carrying his recommendations to the point of action. In a world of large-scale organization, everybody is expected to understand and practice the art of administration. Those who do so effectively will experience a sense of freedom—not in the interstices, but right in the middle of things.

chapter 3

Organizations as systems of human relations

Let us see if we can recapitulate some of the major points made by Mr. Cleveland. In the process of examining them we shall want to add observations of our own derived from some of our recent field research in large organizations.

Perhaps the key to Mr. Cleveland's analysis is his contention that the large organization looks to the casual outside observer like a simple pyramid (or hierarchy, as the sociologist would say). And, unfortunately enough, even some social scientists have also in the same way mistaken the form for the reality. When one gets inside the structures—and Mr. Cleveland himself is a well-qualified participant observer of several such "monolithic structures"—one finds a picture very different from the one the formal organization chart would lead you to expect.

The outward form of both private and governmental organizations is really a reflection of a kind of legal model.

THE LEGAL MODEL

Most traditional human relations, as well as administrative management techniques like "management by result," and elements of organization theory such as the "staff concept" all involve a legal theory of the job of the manager.

Each manager receives from his manager a grant of authority and can therefore be held responsible for certain activities. He, in turn, either directs or cajoles those who are responsible to him to do his bidding. He and they both know what to do because jobs are clearly specified in job descriptions. The manager receives instructions from his superior and passes them on, stopping only to make sure that people do *what they know they are supposed to do and are responsible for doing.* The only possible flaw in the system is illegal action on the part of the subordinate (he ignores or distorts an instruction—an action which constitutes grounds for disciplinary action or additional psychosocial motivation) or the occurrence of a communication break-down (an instruction is lost, misunderstood, or arrives too late). If the manager or his subordinate does what he is told he receives credit in terms of approval or even promotion or increased income; at the least, he avoids receiving symbols of disapprobation.

The hallmarks of this legal view of the organization are discrete entities. Each person has a job to do which has clear beginnings and ends—a job for which he is responsible and by which he can be measured. The individual makes discrete decisions within the confines of his delegated authority.

According to this model, the people on "top" decide what is to be done by establishing broad objectives and plans, and these are gradually converted into more and more specific instructions as orders are passed "down" the line from superior to subordinate. Note how everything is in terms of the vertical dimension!

On the surface, the process of rationalization that endeavors to apply scientific methods to human affairs (as well as to physical phenomena) has proceeded at an ever-increasing pace in these organizations. Not only can production work be segmented "rationally" so that workers can be trained in a matter of minutes or hours to perform preset motions, but the interrelations of machines—and even of engineering drawings to machines—can be programmed so that ideas or plans can be converted "automatically" into action and finished products with little human intervention or decision making. Further, an increasing number of new management techniques such as operations research imply a constriction of human ingenuity in favor of tight control—programmed decision making. The appearance of the organization itself, with its increasing size, levels, and mushrooming standard operating procedures, suggests not only a structural pyramid, but a social mechanism like that which built the original pyramids: a small number of influential planner–decision makers and a much larger number of drones following rigid orders.

REALITY: THE ORGANIZATION AS A SYSTEM OF HUMAN RELATIONS

But as Harlan Cleveland suggests, reality is far different. If we look at the few studies that have been made of how managers spend their time, we find that they devote the greater part of it to *lateral relationships*—not to the superior-subordinate contacts of the organization chart.

With whom do these relationships occur? We recently watched some engineering managers in one very large organization. Here is a partial list of those with whom a manager had to maintain close working relations, quite aside from bosses or subordinates:

■ Groups for whom he is doing work, who have in a sense "contracted out" some part of their activities to him.
■ Groups to whom he, in turn, contracts out work, because they are more expert, or better equipped or staffed to complete the work.
■ Groups from whom he buys parts, materials, or services—some of whom may be within the formal boundaries of the organization, some of whom are outside vendors.
■ Groups who assist him in making such acquisitions or who must prepare facilitating papers, such as purchasing and accounting.
■ Groups who control the usage of or access to equipment, space, and other resources which he must borrow or use in the course of his work.
■ Groups who can help him when he has problems with personnel or with financial or technical aspects of his work, people, or equipment.
■ Groups who ask him for special help in areas where he has technical expertise and can serve as a consultant.
■ Groups who are working at an earlier stage in the overall technology or work-flow process and from whom he will receive ideas, materials, semicompleted designs, or objects for which he must be prepared.
■ Groups to whom he will send what he has processed in the way of ideas, materials, designs, or semicompleted parts, and who want to be prepared.
■ Groups who are doing things in other parts of the organization that

directly or indirectly impinge on his activities and with whom, therefore, he wants to keep in touch.

■ Groups who can help him predict changes in personnel, organization, finances, or level of business activity.

■ Groups who can facilitate his contacts with, and help him comprehend the behavior of bosses, customers, and others.

■ Groups from whom he must secure approval for the work he is doing and his method of doing it. (There may be a dozen or more such groups who audit the activities and accomplishments of the manager in such areas as personnel practices, e.g., the merit increases he gives, the quality of his work, its safety features, or his housekeeping.)

In fact, we can go a step further than Mr. Cleveland. There was a time when so-called staff groups and the union both represented exceptions to the rule that influence and initiation ought to flow down a chain of command. In fact, a good deal of the time of both professors and businessmen was spent trying to justify or comprehend these groups that were off to the side of the organization chart. A manager had to negotiate, or he had to take counsel or advice from such groups, but he didn't manage them or take orders from them.

What we are saying and what research tells us is that most of a manager's relationships in a large organization don't involve authority, a simple "you do this or that." The individual is not caught under the thumb of his superior.

Further, as many observers of contemporary business organizations have observed, the number of internal sources of authoritative decision making is on the increase. So-called staff groups are still proliferating. Experts are added to enable the organization to deal with its potential trouble spots: equipment design, purchasing, personnel, safety, layout and traffic, and countless others. While in traditional (and rarely observed management-theory) terms, these services and skills were to be purely advisory, in actual practice the specialists develop substantial influence and take on a decision-making function. Questions have to be cleared with them for their approval, or for their special processing, and all of this enhanced influence, of course, tends to increase the gross quantity of jobs where initiative and social, intellectual, and administrative ability can be utilized.

A very substantial portion of the relationships of managers, in fact, involves contacts with people among whom there are no clear differences in authority. We should call these lateral relationships—dealings with people who are roughly at one's own level in the organization. And here simple dominance or submission is not important; rather, the individual needs all the skills of persuasion that he can muster.

This is what Mr. Cleveland means when he talks about "learning to work with and in large-scale organizations." These are human skills of the highest order, because of the number of people and groups a man must deal with and the complexity of the relationships—involving, as they do, reduced margins of error and the need for closer coordination among the parts as both technology and society become more complicated.

Simultaneous equations are a more appropriate analog for the organization process than the simple maximization equations of the legal model, which, like the formula of the classical economists, envisions the manager selecting the quantity of each variable he will utilize. The actions of each manager affect all the groups around him, and he must get them to make adjustments before he can shift. As one or another group makes what are for him, the initiator, less than optimal movements, the manager must endeavor to make compensating moves. Of course, these in their turn affect still other groups, and so our peripatetic manager must go around the circuit again, getting new agreements, commitments, and assurances from those he had committed to something else shortly before.

Decision making is thus not a discrete process; it is rather, as Cleveland has called it, a continuous and intricate process of brokerage. As changes take place in the group and in other groups and even outside the organization, pressures are generated which call for responses. The responses are compromises and marginal adjustments reflecting the very different interests and points of view of the parties to the decision. Marketing people may convince top management to give quicker service to customers ordering special lots; but this preference hurts the position of production, which wants to maximize the number of long runs.

We have been trying, in perhaps too verbose a fashion, to present a systems concept of the manager's job which stresses interrelationships as distinct from discrete responsibilities and discriminating behavior. One notably self-assured and successful manager described this process well:

My people get directed (as to what they should be doing) on the basis of pressures: pressures from people doing work for them and for whom they are working and from whom they must get certain approvals. These pressures determine the priorities in a manager's job; they direct his attention; they even force his attention. You see we live on the basis of communication—a man's ability to keep in touch with all the parts of the organization that can affect him.

I have a terrible time trying to explain what I do to my wife. She thinks of a manager in terms of someone who has authority over those people who work for him and who in turn get his job done for him.

You know she thinks of those nice neat organization charts too. She also expects that when I get promoted, I'll have more people working for me.

Now all of this is unrealistic. Actually I have only eighteen people directly reporting to me. These are the only ones I can give orders to. But I have to rely directly on the services of seventy-five or eighty other people in the organization if my work is going to get done. They, in turn, are affected by perhaps several hundred others—and I must sometimes see some of them too—when my work is being held up.

So I am always seeing these people—trying to get their cooperation, trying to deal with delays, work out compromises on specifications. Again when I try to explain this to my wife, she thinks that all I do all day is argue and fight with people.

Although I am an engineer trained to do technical work I really don't have to understand much about the technical work going on here.

What I have to understand is:

1. How the organization works—how to get things through the organization (and this is always changing, of course) and
2. How to spot trouble—how to know when things aren't going well

As for doing a lot of planning ahead—well it's foolish. In fact I usually come to my office in the morning without any plans as to what I am going to do that day. Any minute something can happen that upsets the works. Of course I keep in mind certain persisting problems I haven't been able to make much headway on.

Note the elements our informant has emphasized:

1. A relatively small proportion of time with subordinates
2. Little importance of concepts like authority, power, planning
3. Need for relationships with literally dozens of people—and many of these difficult negotiating contacts

Mr. Cleveland is also astute when he draws the analogy between the body politic and the nervous system. As a political scientist wise in the way of organizations has recently pointed out, the large organization could not exist without the existence of many semiautonomous groups:

In all organizations of any size at all, the flows of materials, people, and messages quickly fall into patterns, or "channels." One has only to make a circle of a hundred points and to connect each point with all the others by a straight line to realize how quickly an unpatterned flow of communications and transportation would break down; even in a small organization, this has the makings of a colossal traffic jam. The simplest way to order these flows is to establish a chain, so that each individual only communicates with two others, but this method is both slow and highly vulnerable to breakdown that paralyzes the entire organization. It is safer, faster, and more economical to divide the members of the organization into groups having individual spokesmen through whom all flows into and out of the group nominally pass, and to gather the spokesmen into groups with spokesmen of their own, thus establishing the familiar pyramidal hierarchical form. The arrangement permits comparatively fast contacts from top to bottom without overburdening anyone, for it reduces the number of contact points considerably; yet it permits most of the organization to continue operations even when part is cut off. The pyramidal distribution pattern of most large organizations develops, in short, because it has significant advantages over the alternatives to it.[1]

[1] Herbert Kaufman, "Why Organizations Behave As They Do: An Outline of a Theory," *Administrative Theory,* University of Texas, Austin, Tex., Mar. 20–21, 1961, p. 47.

chapter 4

Changing employment relationships

For several years, Prof. Margaret Chandler has been exploring the implications of the growing trend toward the contracting out of operations that had been an integral part of the organization.[1] Her research highlights, perhaps more than any other major study, the essentially political nature of the modern corporation, and with it, the emphasis on bargaining, negotiations, and strategy as key elements in interpersonal relations—not just the simple superior-subordinate relations of leadership. For when the parts of the whole organization assume semi-independent status (whether we are talking about an "outside" contractor who has come in to paint the walls or a "service" department that receives more demands for its time than it can handle from departments needing help), the nature of the employment relationship undergoes a major transformation. It would be naïve to ignore this transformation in any consideration of the place of individuals in our large organizations.

[1] I was fortunate to have had the opportunity to participate with Professor Chandler in the early stages of these studies. Cf. Margaret Chandler and Leonard Sayles, *Contracting-out: A Study of Management Decision-making*, Graduate School of Business, Columbia University, New York, 1959.

IMPLICATIONS OF THE TREND
TOWARD CONTRACTING OUT*

In considering the relationship of the individual to the large industrial organization, the experts have a tendency to forget that the firm actually is not the clearly bounded entity that serves as their model for the organizational end of this two-way interaction. Activities of the firm increasingly are being conducted by persons and organizations outside its legal limits. This trend toward assigning work to contractors—toward moving large units of work outside the boundaries of the firm—is ignored by those who still state the relationship between organization and individual in terms of an "inside"-biased view of the world.

Theorists in the field of personnel invariably embed the individual in the matrix of the firm and attempt to find there the means for social salvation and a better way of life. The individual may attain the goal by becoming a member of a closely knit supervisor-subordinate group. The leader of this group will skillfully proceed to change worker unrest into high productivity through his perceptive use of human relations techniques. On the other hand, a number of critics are concerned about the consequences of inordinate coddling, high wages, proliferating fringe benefits, seniority guarantees, and charitable personnel policies. The outcome is envisioned as devastatingly close bonds between firm and employee, and more particularly, between superior and subordinate. In the process of integration the desire for mobility is lessened, along with the incentive to go forward, to incur risks, and to think creatively.

However, the prescriptions of the theorists, whether they tend toward spartanism or hedonism, focus only on the problem of improving internal relations. Even students of automation are concerned primarily with the impact of new technologies on the employees of the automating firm. Problems of job loss and retraining are their major concerns. They ignore the fact that automation also dictates the movement of work to groups outside the firm—to contract forces who absorb the risks attendant upon a period of change and who

* The balance of this chapter is adapted from Part IV, "The Inside and Outside Forces," of Professor Chandler's forthcoming book, *Management Rights and Union Interests*, to be published by McGraw-Hill Book Company, Inc., in 1964.

provide new skills and specialized services, either on a continuing basis or periodically as they are needed. New technologies are making possible the fractionating of processes formerly necessarily conducted by one firm. These advances have made possible the farming out of activities that at one time may have constituted the heart of the internal operation.

Here I want to focus on the impact of the above developments on the relations between the individual and the organization. Contracting out has as its major implication a dramatic shift in the nature of the employment relationship. The industrial manager may become a contract administrator who devotes his time to supervising the work of contractors rather than that of his own forces. Some—and perhaps a large proportion—of the employees on the premises may no longer be on the payroll of the industrial giant such as Standard Oil or General Motors. Instead, they will be employees of the ABC contractors. In some cases ABC will provide a package deal that includes managerial personnel, supervisors, and staff, in addition to rank-and-file workers.

The inside workers and managers thus face not only the threat of automation but also the challenge of the new contract forces who may replace them at any time. Vested interests in both the inside management and the union may discourage moves to contract out in an older plant, but in new plants where there are no precedents to be overthrown, the green light is on for this development. Extrapolating to the future, one can envision a decline in the significance of the durable, shielded relationship between industrial supervisor and subordinate. Employment opportunities will exist as before, but continuity of employment, traditionally furnished by the integrated do-it-yourself industrial firm, will become increasingly a product of a series of agreements held by an outside bureaucrat, the contractor.

The service fields have been one of the major foci for the growth of contract arrangements. As this area tends to be characterized by shifts away from the use of inside forces, we may find it interesting to examine the relationships between the inside service department and the other divisions of the industrial firm, hoping that this analysis will provide clues to the potential impact of new developments. One of the notable findings of my recent research was the indication that 40 per cent of the companies wanted to make some kind of change in service departments that performed the maintenance and construction function. Almost all these plans involved a change in the system of controls by, for example, centralizing, decentralizing, or introducing foolproof priority systems for scheduling jobs. Such changes have an obvious impact on individual managers and workers. With centralization, the service function in separate departments loses out to a combined facility. A new priority system may result in the loss to a service department manager of certain valued sources of support in the company.

This research and that of Dalton[2] indicate that most of the plans for altering the present internal setup are destined to fall short of their mark because they are based on an ideal rather than an actual system of relationships in the establishment. Ideally, of course, the internal service department is well equipped and staffed and efficiently dispatches assignments at the request of the various operating divisions. Moreover, the insiders' intimate knowledge of internal operations should provide the ultimate in intelligent solutions to problems.

The service function is usually described as being both peripheral and supportive. But close examination of the facts reveals that the terms *peripheral* and *supportive* are not the key to the inside service department's position in the firm. In the usual case, for example, where the maintenance department deals with a number of operating divisions, it may become an agent for resolving competition among them. Basically, the service department is a favorite source of organizational slack or leeway, and thus it tends to be used by operating departments as an avenue for bolstering a sagging cost position. Good service and favorable job-cost treatment can place a department ahead of its less fortunate competitors. Reciprocity is involved in this relationship, for in return, the favored department can provide support for maintenance projects and interests. To put the matter simply, operating departments are searching for cost leeway, and maintenance work provides a major source of this commodity. Service work can be obtained at favorable rates; time can be charged to another department's account; or the maintenance budget can serve as a source of funds as department heads share in its appropriations for equipment.

Obviously, however, not everyone can be a recipient of this largesse. The work and interests of those with low bargaining power suffers, and as the backlog of their orders grows larger and larger, pressures

[2] Melville Dalton, *Men Who Manage*, John Wiley & Sons, Inc., New York, 1959, p. 41.

for change build up. But the commodities being distributed continue to be in short supply, and the best that often can be hoped for is a shift in the prevailing pattern of inequitable treatment! In one of the cases examined, a strict priority system had been instituted so that jobs would be done on a first-come, first-served basis, but it did not solve the problem of biased cost estimates and charges or the inequitable charging of time, favoring one department at the expense of another. Moreover, new methods were instituted that effectively circumvented the first-come, first-served system.

This discussion may seem to be designed to prove that the internal maintenance department has inherent venalities, but actually, our real intent is to demonstrate the kinds of organizational processes in which internal maintenance tends to become involved. The extent of this involvement is of course not uniform for all industries and plants. Technological factors provide one significant source of variation. In general, the more fractionated the technology, the greater the service department's ability to remain separate and to conduct shrewd bartering relations with other groups in the firm. In fabrication industries, for example, both parties—operating and service—could interrupt the flow of work without immediate repercussions. Actions of this type are much less possible in process industries (e.g., chemicals and oil refining), where adverse effects are felt almost instantaneously by nearly all departments.

It is clear that the course of the shift from inside to outside as a field of employment relationship is, among other things, a function of the technological organization of the plant. The more "political" the matrix into which the contract relationship is plunged, the greater the expectation that contracting will provide the solution to a variety of human relations problems. The dilemma of the firm described above that cannot cope with the internal political problem effectively may, and in reality does, sometimes suggest a change to contracting out. In fact it suggests an organizational explanation for contracting out. Unable to attack the internal problem effectively, the firm can sidestep it.

In this light, contracting out, substituting outside for inside forces, represents an attempt to solve certain organizational problems. Some of the results of this action will be anticipated correctly; others will not. Some members of management will find advantages in the contract arrangement; others will object to it. The competitive position of some will be improved; for others it will be impaired. When the contractor replaces the inside force, he is inevitably blamed by some managers for harming their competitive relations within the company. Yet, as a result of the contract arrangement, some operating departments are going to expect an improvement in their competitive position; they will attempt to establish relations with the contractor to ensure this eventuality. Therefore, as we examine the role of the inside force in the establishment, we are also constructing the matrix into which the outside force will have to fit.

In order to move inside, some contractors have promised to abandon their traditional independence in favor of conforming and submitting to authority. Others select a strategy of strict neutrality. But as the different interests in management have differing expectations, a contractor finds it impossible to fulfill some without disappointing others. Under these circumstances, neutrality is an equally difficult strategy; the contractor simply is not moving into a neutral environment, and his fate is tied closely to the fate of the management personnel who were instrumental in hiring him. For the inside personnel, the outside contractor provides an extension of communication nets beyond the boundaries of the firm. This resource is often guarded jealously. Other members of management who might regard the relationship with a particular contractor as a diffuse entity—the common property of all—are surprised at the vigor with which the chief engineer may thwart their attempts to contact directly one of "his" maintenance contractors.

Farming out work also involves farming out the relationship with the workers who perform it. Again, the process may appear to be a solution to a difficult internal problem concerning union and management. The organization tells the contractor that there is to be no trouble, and with that the entire matter is placed in his hands. In this way the insecurity of the contractor is passed along to his employees, and the employment relationship is rendered both less secure and less amenable to the customary union pressures. If the contractor's employees show too much spirit, their opportunities of employment may go down the drain, particularly if their activities cause their contractor-employer to lose his contract either through cancellation or failure to renew.

In the initial stages of moving inside, the outside forces will obviously be highly motivated in the direction of compliance with the inside management's wishes. It is easy to extrapolate to a situation in which industrial management regains all of its old "rights" in the employment relationship, while the worker moves back to the days before the Wagner Act. These visions arise precisely because the contractor is brought into the firm for other than strictly technical reasons. To the extent that he is brought in to solve internal political problems and union problems, he may well find that he and his men are trapped in the process. Contractors who are brought in during the transition period from traditional manufacture to partial automation probably will experience the greatest cross pressures in this respect. If and when advanced process technology eliminates the subjective aspects of job performance, tasks may become rationalized to the point where the contractor can replace the inside function without disturbance. Until this time we can anticipate a period of struggle between the inside and outside forces, these groups broadly defined to include members of industrial management favoring either one of these strategies. In the process the nature of employment relations is bound to become the subject of considerable controversy.

chapter 5

Some unlikely sources
of initiative and creativity*

Critics of industrial organization since Marx have argued that machine technology and mechanically paced work have, together with the separation of the worker from his productive tools, led to an estrangement of the worker from his labor and even from himself. While this may or may not be a correct statement of universal applicability, it is doubtful whether the estrangement has extended to the worker's imagination! The evidence is overwhelmingly in favor of the proposition that the worker either has or makes opportunities to act with considerable initiative and even with creativity. I have chosen to review some studies of behavior that I should characterize as creative and indicative of initiative. I am aware that much of what might pass for creativity "bears little relation," as Columbia's Dean Barzun said in a recent magazine article, "to the thing we dignify by comparing it with the act of God." The terms *creativity* and *initiative* conceived as research variables are sloppy; what you call initiative I may call aggressiveness.[1] We had unkinder words for it in the Marine Corps.

* From a previous unpublished paper by Professor Ivar Berg, prepared for the Arden House conference on large organizations.
[1] Conflicting interpretations of initiative and creativity occur in many areas of discourse. Many complain that the ranks of the unemployed—the largest single group of which are Negroes—are swelled by people who lack the spirit of the bird dog, who simply lack initiative. Some of these same individuals are characterized as troublemakers, however, by critics of kennel dogs—when they seek

My creativity, meanwhile, may be dangerous nonconformity in the reader's eyes.

I issue this warning because it is perfectly evident, after even a superficial reading of the literature, that much behavior which is objectively quite indicative of the creativity and initiative of people in organizations is ignored by critics of bureaucracy and of the "organization man." The trouble is that much creative behavior in an organization, much of the initiative exercised by businessmen and administrators in bureaucratic slots, is sometimes condemned in interoffice memos beginning "I take a dim view. . . ." At the same time we express pious concern about declining initiative.

The observation that organizations probably *generate* more initiative and creativity than they inhibit does not seem paradoxical to social scientists. They prefer to make the judgment that creativity and initiative may be expressed in behavior which is inventive, personally fulfilling, autonomous, and performed, as Barzun puts it, "with the common material available to all men." Barzun would add "miraculously" performed. I should not go quite so far, though it may well be miraculous that organizations can both liberate and repress people, particularly when the instruments of organizational repression—reports, ratings, insecure tenure, close supervision—are so numerous, so constant, and so pervasive, while the evidences of liberated creativity and initiative—imagination, skill, courage, and doggedness—are so rare. The social scientist recognizes, too, that "adjustment" and "conformity"—the big devils of the author of *The Organization Man*—are not the only or even the most central of human drives. The fact is that organizations both foster and frustrate the emergence in individuals and groups of autonomous and creative behavior.

Years ago, perhaps in 1912, a symposium on organizations might have been devoted to new ways to make the organization *more* rather than less determinant of human behavior. Frederick W. Taylor, the father of the scientific management movement, was quite persuaded that rational shop organization and careful analyses of work could reduce much individual discretion to tolerable levels, consistent thereby with higher levels of worker efficiency. If there was one central theme in the writings and statements of this applied scientist it was that

---

to attract attention to their second-class citizenship by such inventive alternatives to violence as sit-ins and freedom rides.

soldiering was an unmitigated evil which could and should be greatly reduced.[2] The idea that workers expended effort in avoiding work was not new. Veblen, the iconoclastic economist who coined the term *conspicuous consumption,* wrote a chapter on the subject of industrial sabotage and referred to the tendency of employees to give less than their all as "withdrawal of efficiency."[3] One modern writer has called these employee maneuvers "strategies of independence."[4] This term describes aptly a great variety of organizational behavior; strategy and independence are both involved. The trouble with Taylor was that in his indignation, righteous as indignation usually is in our society, he saw soldiering only as a manifestation of antimanagement attitudes. Such worker attitudes were based on false premises, said Taylor; there was no basic conflict between worker and employer; both should address themselves to making a larger pie instead of fighting over the pieces. It simply did not occur to Taylor that soldiering provided satisfactions beyond those which might accrue from cheating the employer.

Now business leaders may not recognize these strategies as indicative of creativity, but social scientists have been struck by the ingenious responses workers often make, for example, to time and motion studies. In one plant, studied by a group of Cornell investigators,[5] there was a chap named Sam, who was able to burn up drills every time the time-study man reached a speed Sam thought would constitute too tight an incentive rate. The investigators were able to discover that Sam had found a method of grinding his drill whereby it would overheat at much lower speeds than when ground correctly. This example may not gratify those who equate creativity only with company-serving bursts of inventiveness. To the observer who asks the more general question of the impact of organization (in this case its time-study program) Sam's behavior is incredibly creative—from Sam's point of view. His strategy of independence (which, incidentally, kept his work load within bounds that would earn him a comfortable bonus without

[2] Testimony of Frederick W. Taylor, *Bulletin of the Taylor Society,* vol. 11, nos. 3 and 4, June–August, 1926.
[3] Thorstein Veblen, *The Engineers and the Price System,* Viking Press, Inc., New York, 1933, chap. 1.
[4] R. Bendix, *Work and Authority in Industry,* John Wiley & Sons, Inc., New York, 1956, chaps. 1 and 4.
[5] William F. Whyte, *Money and Motivation,* Harper & Row, Publishers, Incorporated, New York, 1955, pp. 15–17.

great exertion, gave him prestige among his peers, and satisfied his instinct of craftsmanship as no mass-produced product could) might not please a Marxist concerned with more fundamental strategies of independence. Conversely, the enlightened businessman, recently enrolled in the cause against the big organization and inspired by a new middle-class humanitarianism, would be hard put to cite Sam's behavior as evidence of organizational repression.

The illustration could be repeated many times over. We are all familiar with the countless shortcuts developed by workers on even the most apparently simplified tasks, sometimes for no other reason than to give variety to a drab shop existence.[6] Ingenious jigs are developed—carefully hidden from methods experts, of course, but ingenious nonetheless. Welders will make bench tools to hold large steel frames plumb while the first key welds are made—tools that can be adapted to different types and sizes of steel frames—tools that will disappear when an assistant department superintendent makes his rounds.

Creativity in the mechanical sphere is only one kind of creativity reported to exist in organizational settings. Employees are equally resourceful in the social sphere. Few informed people today have not, at one time or another, read or heard about the Hawthorne experiments.[7] The researchers found that workers in the Western Electric shops studied in those investigations had developed an amazingly intricate social system wholly outside the organization chart. Social inventiveness, and a liberal quantity of initiative, and no small amount of leadership skill had been combined in the creation of a full-blown society, complete with norms, stratification arrangements, and a highly developed system of justice, violations of which were taken seriously enough to be punished in effective ways. There were, in fact, many full-fledged organizations within the organization, whose goals and methods were often apparently opposed to those of the organization proper. The fact that the investigators looked more than a little patronizingly upon these social networks—as an anthropologist might look at the rites of a preliterate tribe—detracted not one bit from the complexity evident in the world of the worker. Studies like this are usually cited as illustrative of typical patterns of restriction of output in industry for that, in a narrow sense, was what the employees were doing when they fixed

[6] For charming descriptions of such practices, see W. F. Whyte, op. cit.
[7] Fritz Roethlisberger and William J. Dickson, Management and the Worker, Harvard University Press, Cambridge, Mass., 1941.

norms of production—norms which had the force of law and the sanction of custom. But why ignore the creativity of employees because we disapprove of their creations? These studies give little comfort to Marxists who argue that "production relations impoverish social relations";[8] neither do they cause those who equate creativity with increased productivity to jump with glee.

But we need not stop there. We may again fly in the face of conventional wisdom by introducing another phenomenon, the union. Students of local union activity have found that holding union office, handling grievances, and engaging in the political life of the plant provide many individual workers with an outlet for bursts of ambitious creativity.[9] In our concern over union democracy, union corruption, and the power of large unions, we often neglect the day-to-day operations of the local union, remote as it is from the union leader, the sanctimonious congressional committee, the righteous trade association, and the pious editorialist.[10]

The whole process of bargaining is, of course, not uniquely a union phenomenon—there was no union at the Hawthorne plant—but with the advent of unions we have been able to see somewhat more clearly and exactly the extent to which political skills are given an opportunity to blossom. We may not like it when two workers jockey for union office; such democratic procedures often play havoc with a manager's personnel policies, not to speak of his production schedules. But for the candidates, such activities often afford an opportunity to express creative abilities denied in the halls of PTAs with their middle-class norms of language and leisurely debate. One may indeed speculate as to whether many small American communities are not denied the political skills and inventiveness of men who find their appetite for power and negotiation satiated by grievances, arbitration procedures, and daily bargaining between foreman and workers.

A final bit of evidence may be taken from studies of the effect of bureaucratic rules and regulations and of leadership styles. One such

---

[8] Karl Marx and Friedrich Engels, *The German Ideology,* International Publishers, New York, 1947, pp. 3–78.
[9] Leonard Sayles and George Strauss, *The Local Union,* Harper & Row, Publishers, Incorporated, 1953. See also James W. Kuhn, *Bargaining in the Grievance Process,* Columbia University Press, New York, 1961.
[10] For a review of the schizophrenic quality of popular attitudes toward union democracy, see Ivar Berg, "The Nice Kind of Union Democracy," in the *Columbia University Forum,* vol. 5, no. 2, Spring, 1962.

study was concerned with the consequences of a major change from permissive to bureaucratic leadership.[11] The setting was a gypsum company with both a mine and a surface division. After years of comfortable industrial relations but of ineffective production, high costs, absenteeism, and petty pilfering, a new plant superintendent arrived on the scene and proceeded to introduce a series of reforms. Some of them took the form of new rules and operating procedures; others simply involved the strict application of existing rules and regulations. Rules were invoked because the new superintendent could not depend upon established relations with his inherited subordinates to facilitate the new order.

The investigator found that the personnel, particularly those who worked in the mine, differentiated the rules into those they would honor in the breach, those they would honor as advantageous to themselves, and those they would resist with formal acts of independent behavior. The first type of rule, which he called "mock bureaucracy," he illustrated with an analysis of a no-smoking rule which was honored only when insurance underwriters were on the premises. The second type, called "representative bureaucracy," he illustrated with an analysis of safety rules, concluding that such rules are accepted when conformity to them is demonstrably in the workers' interest. The third type was different. He called it "punishment-centered bureaucracy." These latter rules involved a conflict of interest and were caught up as much in the emotions of men as they were in the strange logic of industrial rights. The new superintendent wanted to rid himself of inherited obligations, to recognize the right of workers to bid for jobs.

Now bidding for jobs had been a bureaucratic way by which workers could not only achieve upward mobility in the company but could escape from an unpleasant foreman. The bidding system was incorporated in the company's contract with the union, and its invocation protected the worker in his escape from malevolent authority by reducing the discretion of supervisors: "When a worker bid for and got a job in some other building or division . . . no 'favors' had been done, and no obligations had been incurred."

The new superintendent, in addition to establishing stricter enforcement of rules against informal bull sessions and absenteeism, wished

[11] Alvin Gouldner, *Patterns of Industrial Bureaucracy*, The Free Press of Glencoe, New York, 1954; and *Wildcat Strike*, The Antioch Press, Yellow Springs, Ohio, 1954.

to impose restrictions which would slow down job shifting. These restrictions were rules in which the worker did *not* share a vested interest, and the consequence was a series of actions on both sides culminating in a wildcat strike. The interesting thing about the whole case was the extent to which workers—and later managers—were able to create conditions that made it difficult for the other side to win a clear-cut victory. A healthy dose of bureaucracy was the prescription of the new manager. A self-serving and inventive revision of bureaucratic procedures was the worker's antidote to what he saw as poisonous medicine. Neither side was beaten, and neither side won, because *both* sides were unintimidated by the specter of organization. Both sides saw organization as a vehicle for creatively protecting or advancing their respective interests, and both sides saw frequent opportunities to turn organization to their advantage.

The gypsum-mine study raises an important question. Should we not distinguish between organizational constraints to which members object and organizational features such as safety rules, to which members not only make no objection but give their positive support? Some would argue that an employee does not know his own interests—an argument made by Marxists and paternalistic employers alike—but the question is empirical and cannot be answered by glib ideological assertions.

Critics of the large organization, impressed by mounting costs and the competition between East and West, have argued that we must put a high premium on individual creativity by unleashing it in the ultimate interest of effective national policy. It may offend our sensibilities—especially in our current concern with efficiency and growth—to regard output restriction and grievances as manifestations of initiative and creativity. But if we are concerned with evidence and not self-deception, we ought to recognize creativity when we see it. The critics of the big organization will be at least as hard put to use these cases as evidence for the stifling nature of organization as the biased student will be to ignore them.

I should like to cite some other instances in which the dictates of large organizations have been met with initiative and a measure of creativity. The reader may judge whether the creative acts were consistent with a sense of responsibility. During the pre-World War II era, considerable pressure was put upon middle management in railroads to keep wage costs down. The nation's railroads were faced with growing competition. Highways were being built as were trucks to use them. The airplane came into its own as a peaceful weapon of competition in transportation. Automobile assembly lines were spewing out cars in unprecedented quantities, turning a captive market of rail passengers into a society of drivers. Unresourceful railroad executives tried to compete through low costs rather than through service, efficient organization, and adequate promotion.[12] Adding considerably to the competitive problem was the quasipublic utility status of the railroads and consequent regulation of rail rates. The rails had, in an earlier era, taken advantage of their monopolistic position to discriminate against the shipper who had no transportation alternatives and whose customer status was too weak to command rebates. During this period, meanwhile, unions were beginning to act upon their new freedom, freedom which had come with the New Deal. Middle managers were thus confronted with conflicting demands to keep wage costs down and to keep sufficient peace with labor to enable them to run a railroad.

This double pressure was intensified manyfold during the war, when wages were under Federal control, and skilled manpower was hard to hold. The new defense industries, given impetus by the needs of international conflict, became attractive markets for the skilled worker who wanted high wages and overtime pay to help fulfill the hopes deferred through the thirties—hopes for homes, education, and security. The consequences of these conflicting pressures of the forties and early fifties—and remember we fought another war from 1950 to 1952—now haunt us in every single rail labor dispute. Middle management had risen to the occasion and sometimes in lieu of salary and wage increases, had granted concessions to the employees—concessions which are now condemned as featherbedding and wasteful working rules. To the harried yard superintendent, however, initiative had to be seized and an inventive solution found which would square with the expectations of the home office, the demands of a union leader, the pressures of a seller's market for labor services, and a society conditioned to the general proposition that wages are the sole inflationary force. Concessions were made, therefore, such that workers received what could as easily be called salary substitutes and fringe benefits as featherbedding.[13]

[12] Ernest Williams, "Work Rules and Featherbedding in the Railroads," report presented to the faculty seminar, Graduate School of Business, Columbia University, Fall, 1959.
[13] For a more complete analysis of featherbedding and working rules, see James

Among the railroads the pressures of organization had *generated* rather than inhibited resourceful managerial practices. It was not the yardmaster's fault that these creative adaptations to reality subsequently became permanent aspects of modern railroading, only to be, in the sixties, the theme of ugly ads in anticipation of contract negotiations.

Similar responses can be found within any given organization which uses departmental cost analyses as principal methods for evaluating performance. One very sophisticated student, a California sociologist and business consultant, isolated numerous instances of cost shifting—one variety of a practice known familiarly as "balloon squeezing." [14] This practice was a response to organizational pressures which make competitors out of line-and-staff executives and production and maintenance heads, and which pit one department against its organizational brothers. In the power struggle of the typical organization maintenance foremen are befriended by one executive, and the latter's maintenance costs are charged to another. Committees—the shock troops of so many organizational wars—are formed, and they manage, by a variety of devices, to bring cost figures together rather than apart. The devices include careful efforts not to expose covert evasions and advance notice of inspections. These latter are given a "camouflage of spontaneity" that serves the needs of all. Such practices spare the visiting executives "the unpleasantness of seeing a condition of which they should be officially ignorant, and of feeling embarrassment in possessing knowledge that presupposed corrective action by them." [15] The California sociologist described these practices as "workable illegalities," and they are familiar to anyone who puts his best foot forward in full awareness that his indiscretions are probably not entirely unknown. Many an expense voucher has been filled in with full knowledge that the voucher will be cleared by an "uncritical" comptroller.

Studies of organization in other countries reveal an equivalent genius for solving the problems of organizationally imposed restraints. Both of

Kuhn and Ivar Berg, "The Trouble with Labor Is Featherbedding," in *Columbia University Forum*, vol. 3, no. 2, Spring, 1960, and Jack Stieber, *Hearings before Joint Economic Committee, Congress of the United States*, September, 1959, Part 8, pp. 2597–2628.
[14] Melville Dalton, *Men Who Manage*, John Wiley & Sons, Inc., New York, 1958, pp. 31–35.
[15] *Ibid.*, p. 48.

the leading studies of industrial organization in the Soviet Union describe what the Soviets call *blat*, which may be translated as *influence*.[16] It is applied to all those activities in which the new Soviet bureaucrat must engage if he is to accomplish the goals of an organization in the presence of party surveillance and externally imposed planning regulations. *Blat* involves the use of one's personal contacts to procure materials, tools, and a cloak of legality for the illegal solutions to organizational problems. An alliance with a maintenance foreman in Muncie, Indiana is not different from one with a foreman in Petrograd. Both are evidence of initiative, given the situation of pressure-filled organizations.

These studies of organization and personality, organization and behavior, and finally of what goes on in organizations are sufficient to support the tentative conclusion that while bureaucratic organizations may discipline and dominate, they may also stimulate the individual and the group into inventive solutions and ingenious creations, as well as strategies of independence. It is, in fact, quite likely that while organizations wish, on the one hand, to encourage initiative and creativity, on the other, they seek constantly to contain it. This ambivalence—or contradiction—suggests a more general conclusion: While an organization will take positive steps to elicit and nurture creative behavior and to reward initiative, it is at the same time concerned with the development of mechanisms to prevent independent judgment, the exercise of discretion, and innovation. Hence a company (or a society like the Soviet Union) will invest vast sums in a decentralization program to stimulate leadership and spontaneity at the same time that it will spend considerable money to limit unions or other expressions of employee autonomy.

We might push further in order to formulate two other general conclusions indicated by these studies. The first we may formulate as an answer to a rhetorical question raised by Jacques Barzun: "Should creativity be solicited and encouraged or forged and tempered by the application of resistance and criticism?" The evidence I have cited suggests that organizations probably elicit creative responses in direct proportion to the extent to which they try to limit creativity. In brief,

[16] J. Berliner, *Factory and Manager in the U.S.S.R.*, Harvard University Press, Cambridge, Mass., 1957; and D. Grannick, *The Red Executive*, Doubleday & Company, Inc., Garden City, N.Y., 1960.

the organization itself is a challenge to the inventiveness and resource-fulness of many of the very actors it allegedly represses.

The second conclusion is that the organization is not the only or even the major influence acting upon an individual. Before he is embraced by the warm arms of the corporation and made secure by its bureau-cratic techniques for relieving anxiety, the organization man has been trained by parents, taught by schoolmarms, bossed by sergeants, edu-cated by fraternity brothers (with some interference by professors), and influenced by what sociologists in their poetry call his "peer cul-ture." It is unlikely that the corporation can do more than *select* people who will or will not be creative,[17] or who will or will not be refresh-ingly full of initiative. To presume that the organization can by itself do up or undo the conditions prerequisite to creativity is to assign to organization the creative powers Barzun associated with God.

One could not explain the activities of a former Chrysler president without at least pausing to recognize the basically American nature of the activities for which he lost his job. Bureaucratic organizations in the United States, as one sociologist has pointed out, are "vanguard forms of life in a culture still dominated by a more entrepreneurial ethos and ideology." [18] The auto executive with proprietary interests in a supplier company is making a response affected less by his experience in his organization than by his experience in a society which still makes much of an entrepreneurial *coup d'état.*

We might combine all the conclusions drawn from the evidence by borrowing and paraphrasing a sentence from one of the studies cited:

Intermeshing creativity and conformity, initiative and slavishness is the impossible problem of wedding change and habit. This natural conflict increases to the extent that we are able to fit men perfectly to different functions, for then no one remains to reduce the clash of functions that never interlock automatically or perfectly. . . . Fortunately no one fits his

[17] In addition to the evidence cited in Chapter 7 on the personality-selecting tendencies of organization, we might mention a study by Margaret Chandler which reports that organizations with different "characters" reputedly attract people with appropriate personality traits. See "Garment Manufacture," Case Study no. 3 of *Labor-Management Relations in Illini City,* Institute of Labor and Industrial Relations, University of Illinois, Champaign, Ill., especially pp. 451–455.
[18] C. Wright Mills, *White Collar,* Oxford University Press, New York, 1951, p. 93.

job as well as he should in theory, or we might all be the automatons some novelists and intellectuals say we are becoming.[19]

To this I should like to add only two thoughts. First, we must guard against too great a solicitousness for creativity if by creativity we mean little more than patentable and profitable ideas. Such solicitousness is often transparent and suspect. Second, we should not equate creativity and initiative with happiness. If our goal is to encourage rather than to challenge creativity, we might well be aware that the overwhelming majority of the world's most creative people—including those with material comforts—were most decidedly not happy people. They were motivated, as were the workers at the Hawthorne plant and the distraught managers in the railroad, not alone by a need for happiness but by complex desires which go to the heart of genius.

[19] Dalton, *op. cit.*, p. 107.

chapter **6**

The manipulation problem

Many people for various reasons have participated in the growing outcry about the large organization's use of a variety of techniques to gain greater employee loyalty.

Some critics are just fearful about the growth of the behavioral sciences. They prefer an earlier age when man made no effort to exercise intelligent control over human relations, perhaps a less self-conscious and more romantic period, but one to which most of us would not wish to return.

In many cases human relations has been used or is intended to be used, to manipulate, to adjust people to what the boss thinks is reality, to make them conform to a pattern that seems logical from the top down, to make them accept unquestioningly what we tell them.[1]

The . . . evil of the "human relations" fad is its repeated violation of the dignity of the individual. It becomes a technique for manipulating people. There are certain areas that should be free of the boss's review and his standards of performance. Today, we stick our noses into other people's business, analyzing their motives and judging their lives. We should be able to take a man at face value and not always fret about what he

[1] Peter F. Drucker, "Human Relations: How Far Do We Have to Go?" *Management Record*, March, 1959.

really means. Too many of us are trying to be little tin Freuds . . . consciously trying to be a gentleman. If it doesn't come from the heart, it is phony.[2]

Yet, as Margaret Mead has said, "This is an age where for the first time man has some hope of looking at himself long enough and hard enough to begin to use his intelligence for the improvement of human relations."

Then certain sincerely motivated union leaders see in the growth of more benign supervision and employee-benefit programs a direct threat to the loyalty of their membership and, in turn, the strength of their organizations. As for the latter, they would contend that unions are an essential element in a pluralistic society and that we cannot afford to have a monolithic society:

The personnel program pursues these ends by seeking to induce the worker to accept or adapt himself fully to management's code of values and management's goals. If the worker cannot be molded into a model of the "economic man," he can perhaps be persuaded to acknowledge the propriety of management's efforts to make him one.

Ideally (under such a program) the worker is expected to accept the logic of efficiency and management's right to apply it, unilaterally and without review or approval by the workers. . . .[3]

Prof. William F. Whyte, who was one of the participants in the Arden House conference, has endeavored to evaluate the validity of the proposition that managers can manipulate their employees in devious ways.

ON THE MANIPULATION OF MEN [4]

"Good human relations" is the vogue in industry today. Management is searching for the techniques that will lead to better management-worker relations. And some critics of management are afraid that the search will be successful.

[2] Malcolm P. McNair, "Too Much 'Human Relations'?" *Look*, Oct. 28, 1958.
[3] Solomon Barkin, "A Trade Unionist Appraises Management Personnel Philosophy," in *Readings in Personnel Administration*, Paul Pigors and Charles A. Myers (eds.), McGraw-Hill Book Company, Inc., New York, 1952, p. 16 (reprinted from *Harvard Business Review*, vol. 38, no. 5, pp. 59–64, September, 1950).
[4] The balance of this chapter, except for the conclusion, is by Professor Whyte.

Some management people look back perhaps a bit nostalgically to the day before the union came in and took those worker loyalties away. Now the union is here to stay, all right, but perhaps, through good human relations, management can sell its point of view directly to its employees. Or, if that does not work, maybe good human relations will enable management to sell its point of view to the union leaders and, through them, to the men. The basic aim is to make workers want to do what management wants them to do.

Curiously enough, there are a number of union intellectuals—and some social scientists—who see it in exactly the same way. To them human relations is a management technique for manipulating workers. They warn their fellows—and the workers—against the technique. They proclaim that it cannot be really effective. But they protest so loudly as to betray a fear that the technique might really work. Not that it could eliminate unions, but perhaps—just perhaps—it could so win worker loyalties to management that they would not be prepared to follow resolutely after their union leaders in support of worker interests.

The partisans on both sides might as well relax. Human relations does not provide the tools that some management men hope for and that some union men fear. Nor, according to present trends, does it seem likely that it ever will. The problem is that both sides have misread the research results, if indeed they have paid attention to anything so pedestrian, in the heat of the argument.

It is the dream of some management people to be able to make basic changes in the behavior of workers (and union leaders) without making any really significant change in management behavior. Let's see how this works out.

HOW TO WIN FRIENDS AND INFLUENCE PEOPLE

To such people, the human relations approach covers points like the following five:

1. *Take a personal interest in your men.* Recognize that each man is a unique individual, and show him you are aware of his problems, his hopes, and his fears. Greet him by name. Stop and chat with him now and then, even when the work does not require it.

2. *Provide the worker with information about his job and his com-*

pany. Not too much, of course, but see to it that he gets all that management thinks he should have.

3. *Recognize the status of the individual.* "Make him feel that he is important." The employee is interested in other things besides money. For example, Dale Carnegie reports in this way on the transformation of a skilled mechanic:

This mechanic's job was to keep scores of typewriters and other hard-driven machines functioning smoothly night and day. He was always complaining that the hours were too long, that there was too much work, that he needed an assistant.

J. A. Want (the boss) didn't give him an assistant, didn't give him shorter hours or less work, and yet he made the mechanic happy. How? This mechanic was given a private office. His name appeared on the door, and with it his title: "Manager of the Service Department." [5]

4. *Listen to what the worker has to say.* Management must understand the worker's point of view.

5. *Give the worker a sense of participation.* Consult him on those matters *not* reserved as management's prerogatives.

WHAT PRICE TECHNIQUES?

Those points are all very well as far as they go, but they don't go far enough to make any important difference. Let us examine them, one by one.

1. Does it help to take a personal interest in the men? That all depends. On the sincerity of the interest, perhaps? But what do we mean by sincerity? Surely every supervisor will insist that his interest is sincere. The impression of sincerity depends upon the relationship between smile, nod, and friendly chat and the rest of the supervisor's behavior. Workers have expectations about the sort of other behavior that should go with an expression of personal interest. If the whole pattern of the supervisor's behavior does not seem to be consistent, then workers will class him as a "phony" and the friendly approach will backfire. Let us look, then, to see what sort of other behavior is needed in order to make the friendly approach seem consistent and sincere.

[5] Dale Carnegie, *How to Win Friends and Influence People,* Simon & Schuster, New York, 1937, p. 241 of copy no. 2,365,447 of "the most popular work of nonfiction of our time." (It had reached this figure in 1942. It is still going strong.)

2. Giving workers information is all to the good. But do they get the information they want, or just what management wants them to have? A vice-president for industrial relations in a large company told this story: His company had opened a new plant. After the first month of operations, the plant manager printed in the plant bulletin figures showing how much money the company had lost—hardly a surprising outcome for a new plant. His figures for the second, third, and fourth months were also in the red. However, in plotting the first four months' figures the vice-president noted that, if the trend continued, the plant would finish the fifth month in the black. He looked for these figures in the next issue of the bulletin. He looked in vain. The plant manager circulated no more profit-and-loss statements.

The omission is an amusing commentary on the thinking of some management people. Did the plant manager think that the workers were so stupid that they would not notice the omission? Of course, it was all too obvious. Such actions fortify a common worker belief: that management has an axe to grind and puts out only such information as may help in the grinding.

3. Status is important to be sure, but is made up of more than titles, nameplates, and other physical symbols. You can't make the dishwasher feel important just by calling him a sanitary engineer. (He might like it at first, but he would be embarrassed and resentful when other people laughed at the title.)

We gain status through the way other people act toward us. If they do not act in such a way as to give us recognition, then we have made no gain in status. Symbols such as titles, nameplates, and so on, will help others to recognize our status, providing the symbols seem *appropriate* to the position we occupy and to the job we are doing. Otherwise, not.

Furthermore, in American industry, it is impossible to divorce money from status for very long. Money is by no means the only factor that defines status, but it is certainly an important one. People universally have a feeling that their pay should be in line with the importance of their jobs. I suspect that Dale Carnegie's "manager of the service department" was not contented for long. After a while it probably dawned on him that he was the only department manager who had no one under him and who did all the dirty work of the department by himself. If he did not independently arrive at this conclusion, he probably had coworkers who were glad to inform him about the facts of industrial life. We can imagine them behaving toward him in a manner to suggest this question: "How come you are a department manager, if you are still doing the work of a mechanic?" Eventually he probably went back to his boss to suggest that the new status of manager of the service department called for an assistant (or two), a pay increase, and perhaps even a carpet on the floor.

This does not mean that it is unwise for management to act so as to improve the status of workers. As a worker's importance is enhanced, he is likely to take more pride in himself and his job and to work more efficiently. So management does get something out of its efforts to improve status. But not something for nothing.

4. The ability to listen is a valuable skill, of course. But factory life, to the worker, can hardly be just one catharsis after another. To be sure, there are times when the supervisor can give a man the help he needs just by being a sympathetic listener. But often when a worker talks to a supervisor, he wants to get something done. The worker does not expect the supervisor to adjust his every complaint or accept his every suggestion. But if the supervisor hardly ever responds to the worker's initiative, then the relationship breaks down.

Furthermore, in an organization of any size, the response of the supervisor is often not within his own power. On many problems he will not be able to respond to the worker, unless he can get action out of his own boss. Often this can involve several levels in the chain of command, so that we, as observers, find ourselves dealing with a problem of organization structure.

Listening is a good thing, but—without action—not good enough to reshape the worker-management relationship.

5. Everybody is for "participation"; but what does it mean? Some management people would like to "make the workers feel they are participating" by discussing with them problems of the community fund drive, the company cafeteria, and perhaps even the safety program. But these problems are on the fringes of management's interests, and the workers are well aware of the fact.

ARE YOU PLAYING AT PARTICIPATION?

A few years ago, Rensis Likert's Institute for Social Research at the University of Michigan carried out a notable experiment in participation in two comparable divisions of a large insurance company. In one division, decision making was centralized at a point high above the work level. In the other, an effort was made to bring the decision making down close to the work level through involving the employees in discussions of office problems.

After an initial period of confusion and incredulity, the employees responded with high morale to this opportunity to participate. At first, management was agreeably surprised by the character of the problems the employees brought up for discussion. They did not touch on any areas management considered very important. But, after several months, the discussions shifted toward such matters as promotion, policy, rates of pay, and sharing in cost savings. At this point management decided to limit the scope of its delegation of authority. The "curve of worker decisions soon reached a peak and began to decline." The organization settled back into its preexisting state. The morale-boosting effects of participation were lost.[6]

The problem is that participation tends to lead to more participation. Management cannot expect to limit discussion only to topics that management would like to discuss. If workers are not allowed, and even encouraged, to discuss matters of importance to them, then management might as well call the whole thing off.

Does this mean, as some managers fear, that a real extension of participation necessarily involves a weakening of management control?

Consider the following example of profitable participation in solving a problem:[7]

The Chicago plant of Inland Steel Container Company was facing maintenance costs so high that management was forced to consider contracting out a large part of the work. General Factories Manager Robert Novy, acting for management, took the initiative in calling upon the union for help. After a preliminary look at problems in the department, the union's international representative agreed with Novy that a joint study would be useful. It was clear that the department had complex problems, no one of which could be dealt with in isolation and

[6] From E. Reimer, "Creating Experimental Social Change in an Ongoing Organization," presented at the American Psychological Association meeting, New York, September, 1954. I am indebted to Harold Wilensky for this reference. See his "Human Relations in the Work Place," a chapter in William E. Chalmers et al. (eds.), *Human Relations in the Industrial Setting*, Harper & Row, Publishers, Incorporated, New York, 1956.
[7] See William F. Whyte, *Pattern for Industrial Peace*, Harper & Row, Publishers, Incorporated, New York, 1951.

for which there were no simple solutions. In a one-month period, fifteen union-management meetings were held, reviewing a vast number of details concerning the operating procedures, staffing, and wage rates of the maintenance department. The discussions resulted in a number of important changes in the maintenance department, all the way from a shift in supervisory personnel to a reduction in the size of the work force. The changes—and the discussion leading up to them—brought about improved morale, improved maintenance-production relations, and sharply reduced costs.

Did management lose control in this situation? Do we define control as *the ability to give orders?* Or as *the ability to solve problems?*

BEYOND THE FOREMAN-WORKER RELATIONSHIP

Inland Steel Container's experience suggests another point. It suggests that many plant problems are so large and complex as to be beyond the scope of the individual manager-worker relationship. This has been brought out in two recent research evaluations of supervisory training programs. In each case, the workers under the supervisors who were to be trained were given a questionnaire dealing with their relations with the supervisors before the program began. The same questionnaire was administered some months after the conclusion of the program. The result? Disappointing.

Fleishmann, Harris, and Burtt at Ohio State found that the International Harvester Company program had effected no gain in these supervisor-worker relationships, and that they had perhaps even resulted in a slight loss.[8] The University of Michigan Survey Research Center's study of a training program in two divisions of the Detroit Edison Company showed a small overall gain. It was found, however, that a loss of ground in one division was more than compensated for by a gain in the other.[9]

How can we account for these results? Were the programs in themselves no good? No doubt better training can be given, but probably

[8] *Leadership and Supervision in Industry: An Evaluation of a Supervisory Training Program,* Monograph no. 33, Bureau of Educational Research, Ohio State University Press, Columbus, Ohio.
[9] Norman A. Maier, *Principles of Human Relations,* John Wiley & Sons, Inc., New York, 1952, pp. 184–192.

the programs were a good deal better than the average training courses in industry today.

We find the best explanation in looking at the two divisions in the Detroit Edison study. The researchers found that in the division where progress had been made, the foremen were led by a higher management whose supervision of them was much in line with the principles developed in the course. On the other hand, the foremen in the division which lost ground were under superiors who directed them in a manner entirely out of harmony with the directives of the course.

These findings suggest that the effectiveness of a training program for foremen depends in very large measure upon the pattern of supervision in the larger organization. We cannot improve human relations just through the development of techniques of individual supervisors or managers. We are dealing with large and complex human organizations whose fundamental character does not change just because the supervisor says "Good morning" to the workers.

Only where there is an extension of participation into areas that really matter to workers do they sense a significant change in the character of the organization.

DUAL LOYALTY?

As long as management is only playing at participation, there is no need for its critics to fear that it will gain much ground in the competition for worker loyalties. On the other hand, the real extension of participation does not seem to pose a threat to the union either. The evidence of research so far indicates that in a unionized situation, the effects management desires to attain through participation can be enjoyed only if the union becomes actively involved in the process.

The participation process then builds loyalty both to management and to union. Is this duality a paradox?

Many have assumed that management and union are in competition for worker loyalties—that a gain for management would be a loss for the union, and vice versa. If this were the case, then we would find in our questionnaire surveys that promanagement workers were antiunion and antimanagement workers were prounion. Actually we consistently find, in study after study, that the opposite is true. The promanagement man also tends to respond in a prounion direction; the antimanagement man also tends to be antiunion.

Is this, after all, so strange? What happens to the work level depends on actions taken by both management and union people. Union and management make up mutually dependent parts of the social system of the plant. Workers react to the social system as a whole. Thus, programs initiated by either union or management which aim to solve the human problems of the plant lead to increased worker loyalty to both management and union.

HOW TO FOOL YOURSELF

What then becomes of human relations skills? If we are talking about a set of specific techniques that the supervisor uses to make workers trust him and be loyal to the organization, then these skills may have the value of lubricating the gears of the industrial organization. Similarly, they can be used to lubricate the relations between union officers and workers. But, by the most optimistic estimate, lubrication is all that can be expected from them.

If human relations is to lead to basic changes in worker-management relations, then you have to go far beyond the conception of a package of techniques. You have to think and act in terms of introducing significant changes into such critical areas as managerial decision making, the organization of technology, and the structure of the organization itself. In research, we have seen enough cases along this line to believe that a new managerial approach offers great promise. But this is an area for the venturesome, experimentally minded manager. The manager who hopes, by adding a technique or two to his repertoire, to introduce important changes in human relations, is only deluding himself. He won't fool others for very long.

CONCLUSIONS

A fitting conclusion to Whyte's analysis is provided by a Columbia law school colleague, Adolph Berle, who has commented in a recent volume on our fears about manipulation in the larger context of American life:

There is a persistent tendency to underestimate the capacity, the taste, and the intelligence of the American individual whose choice finally determines the direction of American economic life.

First as to capacity. A spate of literature has conjured up the fear that men may be reduced to robots, manipulated by psychological stimuli. Administrators of the great corporations do endeavor to intervene in private decision making through public relations work, propaganda, and advertising. The impression is created that a "mass man" has come into existence, conditioned to reflexes and capable of being manipulated. A little real science and a great deal of pseudoscience supports this view.

Yet the evidence is not convincing, and it is increasingly less convincing as the level of prosperity, i.e., possible choice available to an individual, rises. Some studies made by Prof. Harold Wolf and Dr. Lawrence Hinkle at the Cornell Medical School are impressive. They analyzed, using the best modern technique, the reactions of Hungarians who had been subjected for more than a decade to the most intense external conditioning processes. The conclusion did not bear out the proposition that men, by any presently known processes, can be deprived (save for the shortest periods of time and then only under conditions like those prevailing in a prison camp) of their inner capacity to determine their own values and to follow a course of conduct based on them. Incidental and temporary variations can be made; but the integrity of the human mind and the human heart cannot be controlled. (Taste presents a more difficult and complex problem. In some measure it can unquestionably be influenced, as most women choosing their fall clothes can testify.)[10]

[10] Adolph A. Berle, Jr., *Power Without Property,* Harcourt, Brace & World, Inc., New York, 1959, p. 136.

PART II

*What are
employees like?*

chapter 7

Do organizations
change people? *

In approaching this question of "what people are like" in terms of their compatibility with the large organization, we may first ask whether there is any evidence that the organization *changes people,* particularly in the direction of making them more pedestrian, less innovative, less willing to take assertive action.

Research on the relationship of organizational experience to individual personality has been more suggestive than definitive. Students generally describe an organization in terms normally used to delineate one or more personality traits, and then they measure the personalities of a sample of the organization's members under the same categories. In the most representative study of this type, two Harvard investigators characterized three organizations as autocratic, democratic, or "transitional" (between autocratic and democratic) according to the way they allocated authority and reached decisions.[1] The investigators then developed scales to measure the democratic-autocratic beliefs as well as

* From a paper prepared by Professor Ivar Berg for the Arden House conference.
[1] D. Gilbert and D. J. Levinson, "Role Performance, Ideology and Personality in Mental Hospital Aides," in M. Greenblat, D. J. Levinson, and R. Williams (eds.), *The Patient and the Mental Hospital,* The Free Press of Glencoe, New York, 1957, pp. 197–208.

personality traits of the organization's members. They found that the personalities and the beliefs varied with the type of organization so that there were authoritarian beliefs held by authoritarian people in the autocratic organization, democratic beliefs and democratic people in the democratic organization, and a mixture of authoritarian and democratic beliefs and people in the transitional organization.

I attempted to repeat and to elaborate upon this Harvard study by studying another autocratic organization in addition to those studied by Levinson and Gilbert and by adding a behavioral dimension to the attitudinal and personality dimensions used in the earlier study.[2] I found, as they had at Harvard, that the personalities of the people fitted in with the character of the organization, and also that behavior was similarly consonant with the organization, the beliefs, and the personalities of the people. In this investigation, personality, belief, and behavior were measured independently.

The difficulty with these studies is that they used crude measures of personality and somewhat intuitive judgments (based upon clinical rather than statistical evidence) about the character of the organizations. This type of study seldom tells us whether the organization "stamped" once diverse personalities, after the fashion of a cookie cutter, in order to ensure an identity between people and organization, or whether the organization recruited congruent types.

I examined this possibility by comparing "old" with "new" members of the organization. I found that there was more homogeneity in personality, in behavior, and in attitude in the seasoned group with long service—in the direction of harmony with the environment—than there was in the newer group. This observation, however, does not tell us directly whether the organization had wrought any change in the senior group. It may be that organizational experience had changed the personalities of the long-service employees. Or it may be that the organizational contemporaries of long-service employees, whose personalities, beliefs, and behavior were "different" left the organization long before my study, either because they were intolerant of an environment unsuited to their personalities or because they were selected out by an uncongenial environment. In short, we do not know whether the organization changed, repelled, and/or selected people or, more likely,

[2] Ivar Berg, "Role Personality and Social Structure: The Nurse in the General Hospital," Ph.D. dissertation, Harvard University, Cambridge, Mass., 1960.

whether all these processes interacted. Only a future study that would reveal whether congenial employees among the short-service group stay or whether the uncongenial ones change, will enhance our confidence that it is possible to study the impact of organization upon basic personality structure.

This particular investigation is especially relevant in the present context in that one of the personality scales I used in my research aspired to measure a personality trait which should be associated, on theoretical grounds, with autonomous behavior. I tried to measure employees' propensities to accept and act upon their impulses.[3] Thus I asked indirectly whether imaginative, innovating, resourceful people were among those who stay or leave the organization, an organization which was not notably hospitable to nonconforming acts of individual judgment and creativity. The organization was a hospital, and while "creative surgery" and "ground-breaking medicine" were proud boasts, it squelched other innovations with very formidable efficiency. New patterns of diabetic nursing care, for example, were restricted. Ingenious systems for simplifying antiquated patient billing procedures met considerable antagonistic pressure, as did other inventive new approaches to old problems.

I found, as I had in examining other personality traits, that there was a close fit between senior members and their organization. Once again the problem of personality change, self-selection, and organizational selection could not be resolved with the data available. The available evidence then does not conclusively support either the "organization man" criticism or the position that organizations have little or no effect on personality.

Other studies are, in their basic design, near carbon copies of the two described, except that some investigators substitute such environments as Indian tribes and universities for more conventional organizations. Results are almost always the same. Thus it was found in a comparative study of Menominee Indians that those who stayed on the reservation, living the traditional tribal life of the Menominee, had personality traits conforming to the social-psychological character of

---

[3] My measure was one developed by Kenneth Kenniston and Arthur Couch of Harvard's psychological clinic. Constructed on the basis of a careful analysis of the mathematical properties of over 100 personality "tests" administered to thousands of people, the two investigators were able to validate their measure in a clinical setting.

tribal life.[4] Menominee who left the reservation were found characteristically to differ from reservation residents in the direction of non-Menominee town dwellers. Again, however, we are not sure whether the Americanized Menominee had changed *after* his acculturation and assimilation or whether he differed from Menominee who remained on the reservation even *before* leaving the reservation.

Many writings on organization and personality, stemming from earlier studies of national character, reflect more a particular intellectual persuasion than a proved theory. Columbia sociologist Robert Merton, describes, in a speculative though suggestive way, what he terms a "bureaucratic personality" and implicitly assigns great force to prolonged experience in a bureaucratic structure as a stimulant in generating tendencies widely alleged to be associated with bureaucrats—rigidity, compulsive preoccupation with rules, impersonality, and acceptance of hierarchical relationships.[5] While recognizing both the logic and the charm of his analysis, we must nevertheless express reservations about this writer's implicit conclusion that priority goes to the organization as cause and bureaucratic behavior as consequence.

We are not prepared to draw any final conclusion on the basis of the evidence then as to the impact of organization on personality. The personality tests used are not demonstrably valid and the fit usually found to exist between men and organizations may grow out of the test used: other traits, measured by other tests, might be found to be *less* typical of a sample of persons in an organization and less closely correlated with the character of the organization. On this score we might anticipate future studies of the impact of organization on personality by those who operate with a more general conception of personality than the one contemplated by the trait approach and who measure personality from its behavioral manifestations rather than from pencil-and-paper tests.

If we can only anticipate future studies of the impact of the organization, we are fortunate in having at present some data on the impact of personality (as measured by specific behavioral indicators of deeper-lying traits) on performance in organizational positions. Unpublished

---

[4] Alex Inkeles, "Personality and Social Structure," in Robert K. Merton, R. Brown, and L. Cottrell, *Sociology Today*, Basic Books, Inc., Publishers, New York, 1958.
[5] Robert K. Merton, "Bureaucratic Structure and Personality," in Robert K. Merton et al. (eds.), *Reader in Bureaucracy*, The Free Press of Glencoe, New York, 1957, pp. 361–371.

research by anthropologist Eliot Chapple and his colleagues indicates that personalities are not randomly chosen to fill organizational positions, that the aggregate of interaction patterns in an organization will be affected by the personalities of role incumbents, and that social structure will be massively influenced by the different qualities of role performance within the behavioral repertoire of people located at strategic positions in the work flow of organizations. Since there is a high correlation between role performance and interaction "style," on the one hand, and personality on the other, and since performance patterns affect social structure, it is entirely reasonable to assume that personality has a considerable impact on social structure. These findings are entirely consistent with those reported in a highly imaginative investigation by Hemphill and his colleagues at Teachers College, Columbia University.[6] In this particular research organizational demands were simulated in a weeklong intensive study of the performance and personalities of over 200 school principals.

Prof. Alex Inkeles, in a careful review of studies dealing with the modern equivalent of the old heredity-environment question, writes of personality and social structure that ". . . both social structure and personality must be treated as important independent but interacting variables influencing the flow of the social process."[7]

[6] J. K. Hemphill, D. E. Griffiths, and N. Frederiksen, *Administrative Performance and Personality*, Bureau of Publications, Teachers College, Columbia University, New York, 1962.
[7] Inkeles, *op. cit.*, p. 267.

chapter 8

The personality-versus-
organization theory*

Over the years, out of the contributions of individuals such as Argyris, Herzberg, Maier, Maslow, and McGregor, has come a consistent view of human motivation in industry.[1] With due credit to Chris Argyris, I should like to call it the "personality-versus-organization hypothesis." I shall state this hypothesis briefly first and then criticize it.

* Adapted from a paper presented by Dr. George Strauss to the seminar in Social Sciences of Organization, University of Pittsburgh, Pa., June 11–23, 1962.
[1] See, for example, Chris Argyris, *Personality and Organization,* Harper & Row, Publishers, Incorporated, New York, 1957; Frederick Herzberg, Bernard Mausner, and Barbara Snyderman, *The Motivation to Work,* John Wiley & Sons, Inc., New York, 1960; Norman R. F. Maier, *Psychology in Industry,* 2d ed., Houghton Mifflin Company, Boston, 1955; A. H. Maslow, *Motivation and Personality,* Harper & Row, Publishers, Incorporated, New York, 1954; Douglas McGregor, *The Human Side of Enterprise,* McGraw-Hill Book Company, Inc., New York, 1960. For an excellent summary of this hypothesis and its application, see James V. Clark, "Motivation and Work Groups: A Tentative View," *Human Organization,* vol. 19, no. 4, pp. 199–208, Winter, 1960–1961. Somewhat the same position is taken by Robert K. Merton in *Social Theory and Social Structure,* rev. ed., The Free Press of Glencoe, New York, 1957, and by Philip Selznick in *TVA and the Grassroots,* University of California Press, Berkeley, Calif., 1949; both suggest that organizational attempts to obtain conformity lead to unanticipated consequences, such as lack of innovation and even rebellion.

THE HYPOTHESIS

1. Human behavior in regard to work is motivated by a hierarchy of needs, in ascending order: physical well-being, safety, social satisfaction, egoistic gratification, and self-actualization. By hierarchy is meant that a higher, less basic need does not provide motivation unless all lower, more basic needs are satisfied, and that once a basic need is satisfied, it no longer motivates.

Physical needs are the most fundamental; but once a reasonable level of physical-need satisfaction is obtained (largely through pay), individuals become relatively more concerned with other needs. First they seek to satisfy their security needs (e.g., through seniority and fringe benefits). When these, too, are reasonably satisfied, social needs (e.g., friendship and group support) take first priority. And so forth. Thus, for example, hungry men have little interest in whether or not they belong to strong social groups; relatively well-off individuals are more anxious for good human relations.

Only when most of the less pressing needs are satisfied will individuals turn to the ultimate form of satisfaction, self-actualization, which is described by Maslow as "the desire to become more and more what one is, to become everything that one is capable of becoming. . . . A musician must make music, an artist must paint, a poet must write, if he is to be ultimately happy. What a man *can* be, he *must* be." [2]

2. Healthy individuals desire to mature, to satisfy increasingly higher levels of needs; in practice they want more and more opportunity to form strong social groups, to be independent and creative, to exercise autonomy and discretion, and to develop and express their unique personalities with freedom.

3. The organization, on the other hand, seeks to program individual behavior and reduce discretion. It demands conformity, obedience, dependence, and immature behavior. The assembly-line worker, the engineer, and the executive are all subject to strong pressures to behave in a programmed, conformist fashion. [3] As a consequence, many individuals feel alienated from their work.

[2] A. H. Maslow, "A Theory of Human Motivation," *Psychological Review*, vol. 40, p. 372, 1943.
[3] These three groups are discussed in Charles R. Walker and Robert H. Guest, *The Man on the Assembly Line*, Harvard University Press, Cambridge, Mass.,

4. Subordinates react to these pressures in a number of ways, most of which are dysfunctional to the organization. Individuals may fight back through union activity, sabotage, output restriction, and other forms of rational or irrational (aggressive) behavior. Or they may withdraw and engage in regression, sublimation, childish behavior, failure to contribute creative ideas, or to produce more than a minimum amount of work. In any case, employees struggle not to conform (at least at first). To keep these employees in line, management must impose still more restrictions and force still more immature behavior. Thus a vicious cycle begins.

5. Management pressures often lead to excessive competition and splintering of work groups and the consequent loss of cooperation and social satisfaction. Or work groups may become even stronger, but their norms may now be antimanagement, those of protecting individuals against pressures from above.

6. A subtle management, which provides high wages, liberal employee benefits, "hygienic," "decent" supervision, and not too much pressure to work, may well induce employees to think they are happy and not *dissatisfied*.[4] But they are not (or should not be) truly *satisfied;* they are apathetic and have settled for a low level of aspiration. They do as little work as they can get away with and still hold their jobs. This unhealthy situation is wasteful both to the individual and to the organization.

7. Some differences in emphasis are found among authorities as to whether the behavior of the typical subordinate under these circumstances will be rational (reality-oriented) or irrational (frustration-oriented). In any case, organizational pressures, particularly the subjec-

---

1952; Herbert Shepard, "Nine Dilemmas in Industrial Research," *Administrative Science Quarterly,* vol. 1, no. 3, pp. 245–259, Fall, 1960; and William H. Whyte, Jr., *The Organization Man,* Simon and Schuster, Inc., New York, 1956.

[4] Herzberg, Mausner, and Snyderman distinguish between *dissatisfiers* (basically, the absence of "hygienic" factors such as good "supervision, interpersonal relations, physical working conditions, salary, company policies, and administrative practices, benefits, and job security," *op. cit.,* p. 113) and *motivators* (basically, challenge, autonomy, interesting work). Similar conclusions are reached by Gerald Guerin, Joseph Veroff, and Sheila Feld, *Americans View Their Mental Health,* Basic Books, Inc., Publishers, New York, 1960. The Herzberg, Mausner, and Snyderman analysis is criticized by Victor Vroom and Norman R. F. Maier in "Industrial Social Psychology," Paul Farnsworth (ed.), *Annual Review of Psychology, Annual Reviews,* vol. 12, Palo Alto, Calif., 1960.

tion to programmed work, may lead to serious personality disturbances and mental illness.[5] Traditional organizational techniques thus not only prevent the organization from operating at maximum efficiency, but in terms of their impact on individual adjustment, are also very expensive to the society as a whole.

8. The only healthy solution is for management to adopt policies which promote intrinsic job satisfaction, individual development, and creativity, according to which people will willingly and voluntarily work toward organizational objectives because they enjoy their work and feel that it is important to do a good job.[6] More specifically, management should promote job enlargement, general supervision, strong, cohesive work groups, and decentralization. In a nutshell, management should adopt what Harold Leavitt calls "power-equalization techniques."

CRITICISM

The view expressed above is, in a sense, a hypothesis as to human behavior in organizations. But it is more than a coldly objective hypothesis: It is a prescription for management behavior, and implicit in it are strong value judgments.[7] With its strong emphasis on individual dignity, creative freedom, and self-development, this hypothesis bears all the earmarks of its academic origin.

Professors place high value on autonomy, inner direction, and the quest for maximum self-development. As much as any other group in

[5] Recent evidence suggests that unskilled workers are significantly more likely to suffer from personality disturbances and psychosomatic illnesses than are skilled workers, and that these differences become manifest only after the individuals take up their work. (In other words, once individuals land in unskilled jobs, they tend to become more maladjusted.) Arthur Kornhauser, "Mental Health of Factory Workers: A Detroit Study," *Human Organization*, vol. 21, no. 1, pp. 43–46, Spring, 1962; John R. P. French, Jr., Robert L. Kahn, and Floyd C. Mann (eds.), "Work, Health and Satisfaction," *The Journal of Social Issues*, vol. 18, no. 3, July, 1962.

[6] Perhaps the most general statement of this position is McGregor's Theory Y. See McGregor, *op. cit.*

[7] There seems to be a certain amount of confusion as to whether prescriptions for power equalization are written from the point of view of organizational efficiency or mental health (and possibly the degree of confusion has increased since the primary source of research funds in this area has shifted from the military to the National Institute of Mental Health). There are those who claim that what is good for the individual will, in the long run, be good for the organization, and vice versa. Nevertheless, it is useful to keep one's criteria explicit.

society, their existence is work-oriented; for them, creative achievement is an end in itself and requires no further justification. Most professors are strongly convinced of the righteousness of their Protestant ethic of hard work and see little incongruity in imposing it upon the less fortunate.

And yet there are many misguided individuals (perhaps the bulk of the population) who do not share the professors' values and would not be happy in a professor's job. Further, the technical requirements of many lines of work are very different from those of academia. Academic work is best accomplished by those who adhere to academic values, but it is questionable whether these values are equally functional in other lines of work, where creativity is not required to get the job done, but only the ability to follow orders.

In the pages which follow, I shall seek to reevaluate the personality-versus-organization hypothesis. I shall suggest, first, that it contains many debatable value judgments and, second, that it ignores what Harold Leavitt has called "organizational economics." I shall conclude that a broad range of people do not seek self-actualization on the job —and that this may be a fortunate thing, because it might be prohibitively expensive to redesign some jobs to permit self-actualization.

VALUE JUDGMENTS

It seems to me that the hypothesis, as often stated, overemphasizes (1) the uniqueness of the personality-organization conflict to large-scale industry, (2) the universality of the desire to achieve self-actualization, and (3) the importance of the job (as opposed to the community or the home) as a source of need satisfaction. Too little attention is given to economic motivation.[8]

The uniqueness of the problem

At least some authors seem to overdramatize the personality-organization conflict as something unique to large-scale organization (particu-

---

[8] I must confess that many of these criticisms apply to my own writing. See George Strauss and Leonard R. Sayles, *Personnel: The Human Problems of Management,* Prentice-Hall, Inc., Englewood Cliffs, N.J., 1960, especially chaps. 4–8 and 12, chapters for which I was responsible. See the review by Arthur Brayfield, "Treating Faint Workers," *Contemporary Psychology,* vol. 2, no. 3, pp. 92–93, March, 1962.

larly to mass-production industry). But this conflict is merely one aspect of what has been variously characterized as the conflict between individual and society, individual and environment, desire and reality, id and super ego. "Thus the formal organization . . . is not truly the real villain; rather any kind of organized activity, from the most democratic to the most authoritarian, contains within itself the necessary conditions for conflict." [9]

Similarly the impact of the industrial revolution on work satisfaction can be overemphasized. Much is made of "alienation" (dictionary meaning: *turning away*) from work. Comparisons are constantly made between the old-time craftsman who did the entire job and the mass-production worker of today. But I doubt whether the medieval serf or the Egyptian slave enjoyed much sense of autonomy or creativity (though, one might perhaps argue that he had more of a sense of identification and less of a feeling of anomie than does his better-fed modern counterpart). Perhaps there is less job satisfaction today than there was 100 years ago. Obviously no objective ways can be devised to measure this change, but my surmise is that the turning away has been less dramatic than some have suggested. Boring, programmed jobs have existed throughout history.

Others are as skeptical as I am of the theory of increased alienation. In his conclusion to a survey of job-satisfaction studies, Robert Blauner questions

. . . the prevailing thesis that most workers in modern society are alienated and estranged. There is a remarkable consistency in the findings that the vast majority of workers, in virtually all occupations and industries, are moderately or highly satisfied, rather than dissatisfied with their jobs. . . . The real character of the [pre-mass production] craftsman's work has been romanticized by the prevalent tendency to idealize the past. . . .[10]

And J. A. C. Brown asserts that "in modern society there is far greater scope of skill and craftsmanship than in any previous society." [11]

[9] Warren G. Bennis, "Leadership Theory and Administrative Behavior," *Administrative Science Quarterly*, vol. 4, no. 3, p. 281, December, 1959. Ironically, some of those most concerned with the tyranny of the organization would substitute for it the tyranny of the participative group.
[10] "Work Satisfaction and Industrial Trends in Modern Society," in Walter Galenson and Seymour Martin Lipset, *Labor and Trade Unionism*, John Wiley & Sons, Inc., New York, 1960, pp. 352–353.
[11] J. A. C. Brown, *The Social Psychology of Industry*, Penguin Books, Inc., Baltimore, 1954, p. 207.

The universality of the desire for self-actualization

The basic hypothesis implies a strong moral judgment that people should want freedom and self-actualization,[12] that it is somehow morally wrong for people to be lazy, unproductive, and uncreative. It seems to me that the hypothesis overemphasizes individuals' desires for freedom and underemphasizes their desire for security. It can even be argued that some of the personality-versus-organization writing has a fairly antisocial, even nihilistic flavor; it seems to emphasize individual freedom and self-development as the all-important value. Yet mature behavior does not mean freedom from all restrictions; it means successful adjustment to them.

As Erich Fromm has suggested, most people don't want complete freedom. They want to know the limits within which they can act (and this is true both on and off the job). To put it another way: Most people are willing to tolerate and may even be anxious for a few areas of their lives to be unpredictable and exciting, but they insist that in a majority of areas events should occur as expected. The research scientist, for example, may relish the novelty and uncertainty of laboratory work, but he insists that his secretary always be on call, that his technician give predictable responses, and that his car start with complete regularity.

True, some people seek much less confining limits than do others, and some are not too upset if the limits are fuzzy. Many, however, feel most comfortable if they work in a highly defined situation. For them freedom is a burden; they want firm, secure leadership. And many more, if not fully happy with programmed work, accommodate to it rather easily.

Argyris, for example, might reply that such individuals are immature personalities who have adjusted to organization restrictions by becoming apathetic and dependent; were the organization environment healthy, these individuals would react differently. But in many cases the restrictions which conditioned these people occurred in childhood or are present in the culture. Such individuals may be too far gone in dependence to react well to power equalization, and their attitude is not likely to be changed short of intensive psychotherapy. Indeed many people may have internalized and made part of their self-concept a low

---

[12] Though the concept of self-actualization seems penetrating, I tend to agree with Bennis that it "is, at best, an ill-defined concept . . . [and that] self-actualized man seems to be more myth than reality," *op. cit.*, p. 279.

level of aspiration regarding their on-the-job responsibilities and their ability to handle them. What psychologists call the "theory of dissonance" suggests that sudden attempts to increase their sense of autonomy and self-determination might be quite disturbing.

Impressive evidence of the need for self-actualization is provided by the preliminary results of the mental-health studies which suggest that poor mental health is correlated with holding low-skilled jobs. And yet the evidence is still not complete. Apparently not everyone suffers equally from unskilled work, and some adjust more easily than others. (Perhaps these studies will help us to improve the prediction process, so that we can do a better job of selecting and even training people for this kind of work.)

Further, it is far from clear whether this lower mental health is caused primarily by the intrinsic nature of unskilled work, or by the fact that such work pays poorly and has low status both off and on the job.[13] In so far as mental disturbances are caused by economic and social pressures at home, higher wages may be a better solution than improved human relations on the job or a rearrangement of work assignments.

A hasty glance at the research in this field, as summarized in two reviews,[14] makes it abundantly clear that unskilled workers are not the only ones who suffer from poor mental health. Depending on which study one looks at or what mental-health index is used, one can conclude that executives, clerical personnel, salespeople, and lower-level supervisors all suffer from below-average mental health. The evidence makes one sympathize with the old Quaker, "All the world is queer save me and thee; and sometimes I think even thee is a little queer."

[13] Both the Wayne State and the Michigan studies emphasize that no single factor explains the relationship. Kornhauser concludes (op. cit., p. 46): "Both on rational grounds and from empirical evidence, I see no reason to think that it is useful to single out one or a few of the job-related characteristics as distinctly important. . . . If we are to understand why mental health is poorer in less-skilled, more routine factory jobs, we must look at the entire pattern of work and life conditions of people in these occupations—not just at single variables."

[14] Stanislav V. Kasl and John R. P. French, Jr., "The Effects of Occupational Status on Physical and Mental Health," Journal of Social Issues, vol. 18, no. 3, pp. 67–89, July, 1962; Vroom and Maier, op. cit. See also Guerin, Veroff, and Feld, op. cit., p. 162.

The job as the primary source of satisfaction

There is an additional value judgment in the basic hypothesis that the *job* should be a primary form of need satisfaction for everyone (as it is for professors). But the central focus of many people's lives is not the job (which is merely a way of getting a living), but the home or the community. Many people find a full measure of challenge, creativity, and autonomy in raising a family, pursuing a hobby, or taking part in community affairs. As Robert Dubin puts it:

> Work, for probably a majority of workers, and even extending into the ranks of management, may represent an institutional setting that is not the central life interest of the participants. The consequence of this is that while participating in work a general attitude of apathy and indifference prevails. . . . Thus, the industrial worker does not feel imposed upon by the tyranny of organizations, company, or union.[15]

In my own interviewing experience in factories, I often ran across women who repeated variants of, "I like this job because it gets me away from all the kids and pressures at home." One girl even told me, "The job is good because it gives me a chance to think about God." Such individuals may feel little need for power equalization.

In any case, as Kerr, Harbison, Dunlop, and Myers predict, work, in the future, will doubtless be increasingly programmed and will provide fewer and fewer opportunities for creativity and discretion on the job.[16] On the other hand, the hours will grow shorter, and there will be a "new bohemianism" off the job. All this suggests the irreverent notion that *perhaps* the best use of our resources is to accelerate automation, shorten the workweek just as fast as possible, forget about on-the-job satisfactions, and concentrate our energies on making leisure more meaningful.

Underemphasis on economic rewards

At the same time that the hypothesis overemphasizes the job as a source of need satisfaction, it also underemphasizes the role of money

---

[15] "Industrial Research and the Discipline of Sociology," *Proceedings of the 11th Annual Meeting, Industrial Relations Research Association*, Madison, Wis., 1959, p. 161.
[16] Clark Kerr, John T. Dunlop, Fredrick H. Harbison, and Charles A. Myers, *Industrialism and Industrial Man: The Problems of Labor and Management in Economic Growth*, Harvard University Press, Cambridge, Mass., 1960.

as a means of motivation. The hypothesis says that once employees obtain a satisfying level of economic reward they go on to other needs and, presumably, are less concerned with money. However, the level of reward which is *satisfying* can rise rapidly over time. Further, money is a means of satisfying higher needs, too—ego, safety, and, for some, even self-actualization, e.g., the individual who (perhaps misguidedly) seeks to live his life off the job engaging in "creative" consumption. True, employees expect much better physical, psychological, and social conditions on the job today than they did fifty years ago. But they also expect more money. There is little evidence that money has ceased to be a prime motivator.

"ORGANIZATIONAL ECONOMICS"

Perhaps the most fundamental criticisms of the personality-organization hypothesis is that it ignores (or at least misapplies) "organizational economics," that is, it fails to balance carefully the costs and gains of power equalization. To be sure, most power-equalization advocates point out the hidden costs of autocracy: apathetic and resentful employees, turnover, absenteeism, sabotage, resistance to change, and all the rest. Traditional forms of supervision may be expensive in terms of the lost motivation and energy which might have been turned to organizational ends; they are even more expensive in terms of mental health. Yet some writers, in their moments of wilder enthusiasm, tend to overestimate the gains from what they propose and underestimate the costs.

The gains from power equalization

It is argued that traditional organizational methods lead either to dissatisfaction, anxiety, and aggression or to dependency, conformity, and doing only a minimum of work—and that these problems would be reduced by power equalization.

Carried to excess, anxiety and aggression are undoubtedly harmful both to the organization and the individual. But many psychological studies suggest that dissatisfaction and anxiety (and even aggression, depending on how it is defined) spur individuals to work harder. Autocratic, work-oriented bosses very often get out high production;

on occasion, their subordinates even develop high morale and cohesive work groups.[17]

Still, beyond certain limits, dissatisfaction, anxiety, and aggression are not in the organization's interests. There is much more doubt about apathy and conformity. It is often argued that an apathetic worker who is subject to "hygienic" supervision will work only enough to avoid getting fired, that he will never exercise creativity or imagination or execute an outstanding performance. On many jobs, however, management has no use for outstanding performance. What is outstanding performance on the part of an assembly-line worker? That he works faster than the line? That he shows creativity and imagination on the job? Management wants none of these. *Adequate* performance is all that can be used on the assembly line and probably on a growing number (I know no figures) of other jobs in our society. Here the conformable, dependent worker may well be the best.[18] As Leavitt and Whisler put it, "The issue of morale versus productivity that now worries us may pale as programming moves in. The morale of programmed personnel may be of less central concern because less (or at least a different sort of) productivity will be demanded of them." [19]

Even at the management level, there may be an increasing need for conforming, unimaginative types of "organization men," if the future verifies Leavitt's and Whisler's prediction that "jobs at today's middle-management levels will become highly structured. Much more of the work will be programmed, i.e., covered by sets of operating rules governing the day-to-day decisions that are made." [20] Despite *The Organization Man* it might be argued that nonconformity will be useful to the organization only in increasingly limited doses.

[17] For a list of the conditions under which "authoritarian leadership might be as effective as its alternatives," see Harold L. Wilensky, "Human Relations in the Workplace," Arensberg and others (eds.), *Research in Industrial Human Relations,* Harper & Row, Publishers, Incorporated, New York, 1957, pp. 25–50. Interestingly, the personality-organization hypothesis is strongly influenced by Freud. Yet Freud postulated that "productive work is partially a function of the expression of hostility to the leader" (Bennis, *op. cit.,* p. 292).

[18] For an outstanding example see William J. Goode and Irving Fowler, "Incentive Factors in a Low Morale Plant," *American Sociological Review,* vol. 14, no. 5, pp. 619–624, October, 1949.

[19] Harold Leavitt and Thomas Whisler, "Management in the 1980s," *Harvard Business Review,* vol. 36, no. 6, p. 46, November, 1958.

[20] *Ibid.,* p. 41.

The costs of power equalization

On the other hand, power equalization can be quite costly to the organization. To make general supervision or participative management work, many of the old-line autocratic supervisors must be retrained or replaced; this is a costly process, which may result in the demoralization or elimination of the organization's most technically competent individuals. It is extremely difficult to develop internalized motivation on many routine jobs; once the traditional, external sanctions (for example, monetary rewards and fear of discharge) are removed, *net* motivation may fall on balance. And it is fairly meaningless to talk of delegation of authority to assembly-line workers or girls on a punch-card operation; the very nature of the technology requires that all essential decisions be made centrally.

"But if the nature of the job makes power-equalization techniques impractical," some may argue, "change the nature of the job." Rensis Likert puts this well:

To be highly motivated, each member of the organization must feel that the organization's objectives are of significance and that his own particular task contributes in an indispensable manner to the organization's achievement of its objectives. He should see his role as difficult, important, and meaningful. This is necessary if the individual is to achieve and maintain a sense of personal worth and importance. *When jobs do not meet this specification they should be reorganized so that they do.*[21]

True, there are many opportunities to redesign jobs and work flows so as to increase various forms of job satisfaction such as autonomy and achievement.[22] But whether such changes should be made is a matter for organization economics.

These changes, when accompanied by appropriate forms of supervision and proper selection of personnel, may sometimes result in substantial increases of productivity. (Purely technological losses in

[21] Rensis Likert, *New Patterns of Management,* New York, McGraw-Hill Book Company, Inc., 1960, p. 103. (The italics are my own.)
[22] See, for example, Louis E. Davis and Richard Werling, "Job Design Factors," *Occupational Psychology,* vol. 34, no. 2, pp. 109–132, April, 1960; Georges Friedmann, *Industrial Society,* The Free Press of Glencoe, New York, 1955; Eliot D. Chapple and Leonard R. Sayles, *The Measure of Management,* The Macmillan Company, New York, 1961; Strauss and Sayles, *op. cit.,* chaps. 2 and 16.

efficiency may be more than offset by increased motivation, less work-flow friction, and the like.) Obviously, in such instances organizational economics would dictate that the changes should be introduced.

But in other areas technological changes can be made only at a substantial cost in terms of productivity—and the impact of automation and information technology seems to be increasing the number of jobs where change would prove costly. Should we scrap the advances of technology in these areas in order to foster good human relations? Or should we say "Thank God for the number of people who have made an apparent adjustment to routine jobs. Would that there were more!"? Perhaps—as has been suggested earlier—it would be best to devote our resources to shortening the workweek continuously and helping people to enjoy their leisure more fully.

Considerable evidence leads to the conclusion that a relatively stable situation can exist, in which workers perform relatively routine, programmed jobs under hygienic supervision.[23] Though these workers may not be satisfied (in the Herzberg sense) and may be immature, apathetic, and dependent (in the Argyris sense), they are not actively dissatisfied; they do not feel a need for additional responsibility; and they seek meaning in life from their home and community rather than from their job. To be sure, these individuals are maximizing neither their productive efforts nor their possible job satisfaction. But both management and employees find the situation suffices their needs. Barring sudden change, it is stable. It may well be the best we are likely to get in many situations without costly changes in such important matters as technology and child upbringing.

SUMMARY

My concern has been with the personality-versus-organization hypothesis. I have tried to demonstrate:

1. Though many individuals find relatively little satisfaction in their work, the absence of gratification may not be so great a deprivation as the hypothesis would suggest, since many of these same individuals center their lives off the job and find most of their satisfaction in the community and the home. For these individuals power equalization may not liberate much energy.

[23] For example, Chris Argyris, *Understanding Human Behavior*, Richard D. Irwin, Inc., Homewood, Ill., 1960, chap. 5.

2. Individuals are not motivated solely to obtain autonomy or self-actualization. With various degrees of emphasis, individuals also want security and the knowledge of what is expected of them. Power equalization may certainly stir up a good deal of anxiety among those who are not prepared for it, and at least some individuals may be reluctant to assume the responsibility it throws upon them.

3. Power-equalization techniques have little meaning when management needs no more than an adequate level of production, as is often the case when work is highly programmed. Under such circumstances the costs entailed by modification in job design and supervisory techniques may be greater than the gains obtained from increased motivation to work.

All of the above does not mean either that the personality-versus-organization hypothesis is meaningless or that power-equalization techniques are not useful. Quite the contrary. What it does mean is that many individuals can accommodate themselves to the demands of the organization without too much psychological loss, and that for them the personality-organization conflict is not particularly frustrating. Similarly, in many circumstances the gains to the organization from power equalization may be moderate and more than offset by its costs.

For other individuals (for example, scientists working in large companies) the personality-organization conflict may be felt quite acutely. For the most part they are the very individuals whose work cannot be programmed and from whom management wants more than merely adequate production.

Our summary reemphasizes the often-made point that no single style of leadership can be universally appropriate. The techniques which work on the assembly line will almost certainly fail with research scientists. Indeed it is fair to predict that, over time, the differences among supervisory styles may increase. Perhaps in the future we shall have at one extreme research scientists and others doing creative work, who will be putting in a forty-hour or longer workweek under conditions of relative power equalization. At the other extreme may be those who submit to close supervision on highly programmed jobs, but for only twenty hours or so. Shades of *Brave New World:* the alphas and gammas!

chapter 9

What people want from their jobs: impact of our changing culture

Dr. Strauss has laid bare one favorite misconception of Americans by Americans. Apparently we are inclined to think that as individuals we are much like the stereotype of the pioneer on the frontier. Aren't we all overflowing with initiative, anxious to make our own way and to take what risks we must? And aren't we held back just by the lack of adequate supply of positions that call for these characteristics?

CHANGING NORMS GOVERNING EMPLOYEE BEHAVIOR

There are many values or norms, as the social scientist would say, that circulate in our culture and shape our evaluation of contemporary institutions like business and all large organizations. For example, the typical American is considered a storehouse of initiative, and there is some consensus of opinion on the ideal size of any human group.

Americans still tend to think back to their rural, small-town past and to idealize the relationships that they assume were characteristic of that earlier period. They value highly the small, primary group where members shared identical views on most subjects and the individual was supported by this assured consensus and a network of intimate, familylike relationships. They usually fail to recognize that groups of this kind did not necessarily foster individual initiative,

81

autonomy, and self-assertion. But since many mutually contradictory norms can exist in a society, this failure always to realize the ideal is no surprise for us.

In contrast the large, impersonal, rational business organization can seem most threatening. These large "secondary" groups lack the unity of objective, the closeness of familylike feelings, and the mutual support identified with rural America.

One could criticize this predilection for smallness, arguing that prejudice, a sense of confinement, nepotism, and debilitating paternalism all thrive in the smaller group, whether it is a town or the family-owned and -operated company—but that is not really relevant here. The important point is simply that we have, with good historical reasons, a built-in bias, which gives us an image of the "good," "typical" employee and company.

As we noted in Chapter 1, critics often contend that the organization is becoming too grasping—exerting centripetal force to tie the individual egoistically and socially to itself, as well as imposing the more traditional economic constraints. As evidence it is easy to muster quantitative indices of the growth of seniority benefits of all kinds, pension plans, and deferred compensation. In addition to direct economic rewards for sustained loyalty, the firm presumably seeks, through social-psychological techniques, to focus the individual's interests on itself. Recreation programs and a host of communication-technique ceremonials that integrate breadwinner and family into the company can be cited.

But, on the other side, is it not conceivable that these centripetal forces are just reactions to the growing strength of centrifugal forces in the environment and that the organization is seeking to retain an older equilibrium, rather than a redistribution of the forces?

Look for a moment at the community forces driving the individual away from complete identification with the firm. Geography and population distribution are obvious factors. The typical firm of an earlier period was located in a small community where every conceivable tie bound the employee to the firm and the community. As in the famous "Yankee City" study of Newburyport, Massachusetts, the role of the employee-boss in the factory was reinforced by his social position in the community.[1] Further occupational stratifications in the factory had

---

[1] Lloyd Warner and J. O. Low, *The Social System of the Modern Factory*, Yale University Press, New Haven, Conn., 1947.

complementary significance in the wider community. The worker's status-age grading and the boss's status were paid for in the same currency in the plant and in the town.

Urban areas, whether suburban sprawls or megalopolitan spreads, provide no such integration. Identifying the company, its owners or managers or occupational structure, with the community (with the exception of one-industry towns) is next to impossible. The individual feels no tie to the organization based on community reinforcements—unless the firm itself takes special pains to create it.

Changes in the employee's conception of the relative importance of work, his role in marriage and the home, is complicating the picture of a shifting urban-rural balance in the United States. As George Strauss has indicated in Chapter 8, leisure-time pursuits may be valued more highly than work objectives; the home more than the career. A companionate-colleague marriage, in which both parties share in the activities of child rearing and house tending, may lead, as Margaret Mead notes in the material to follow, to the "tired father in the office" as distinct from the fatigued businessman in the home! An optimistic, affluent society, with an increasing number of economic-security features built in, may also discourage the individual's concern with long-run occupational goals. Of course, it would be foolhardy to speculate on optimizing the degree of economic insecurity, but it is just as naïve to ignore the growing list of centrifugal forces in the community and in contemporary culture.

As an anthropologist and student of contemporary culture, Dr. Margaret Mead has been concerned with the kinds of attitudes and ideals that individuals bring with them into the organization. Several years ago, we were very fortunate in having her as our guest at a Columbia function. Her observations are most relevant to the questions we have been considering.

HIS FAMILY LOOKS AT THE BUSINESSMAN[2]

How does our society picture the businessman? We mean the businessman in relation to the woman he marries, to the women his associates

[2] This section is drawn from an edited tape of the remarks of Dr. Mead as printed in the *Alumni Newsletter* of the Graduate School of Business of Columbia University, January, 1958.

marry, to his children, to his neighbors, and to the community in which his family lives.

The businessman we used to know stayed late at the office; he even stayed at the office on Saturday. He was always tired when he came home. He paid liberally for his wife's culture and his children's education, but he took no part in either of them. Today, as young people consider what career they are going to follow, and whether they are going to go into business, they are burdened with this picture of the past. It clashes very strongly with most of the things that young people want out of marriage today, because our present image of the family is based on the belief that it should not be secondary in a man's time and interest.

Remember, I'm not saying that this is what the businessman was. Most businessmen were very much interested in what they were doing, and they weren't only interested in money. Money was just the measure of what they were doing, and their success. (If you talked to poets you would think they weren't interested in anything but publication.) Of course businessmen were interested in building up a company, in merging companies, and in new processes, and they still are. These were the things they talked to each other about, but they were firmly convinced they couldn't talk to anybody else about such matters. Businessmen have been taught for two or three generations that they can't express themselves, and if they do they will make a mistake about "art" and "culture." So they are an extraordinarily silent and inexpressive group of people outside their own field, where they speak with great competence.

To understand this picture of the businessman, we have to add the notion that if you go into business and really work hard, you work yourself to death. You get ulcers. This idea has been growing now for the past twenty years. In the contemporary climate of opinion, young people's notion of life is that it shouldn't be spent in working a long, long time for results that come later. They all want to get married very young and have four or five children as soon as possible, and they are not willing to work for rewards that come only at the end of the proceedings.

This is just what the businessman used to do. He worked and worked, and then if he didn't die, he would travel. He was not supposed to be enjoying life at all during the years when he was making his pile. The picture was that he always started in abject poverty and that his wife sympathized with him and worked with him. She suffered and scrubbed, and he usually outgrew her later. This is again not true. This is the stereotype.

Now if you look at this picture of a life in which you do something that is of no interest to other people, where you exhaust yourself working in order to make money for a wife and children you don't see and for an old age you won't get, you understand why this is extremely repellent to our young people today.

And we're getting a counterimage that is perhaps just as dangerous. We used to have the tired businessman at home; now we have the tired young father at the office. The young manager is expected to spend an enormous amount of time with his wife and children, and to come home fresh.

There is also the question of "fresh for what?" We have more highly paid, volunteer, manual labor in the United States today (plumbing, lawn mowing, and the like), than has ever existed before. Historically, when a man got important enough to be a vice-president, a chief justice, or an executive, somebody else mowed the lawn. And always in history somebody else took care of the baby. We are the first civilization that has ever risked putting responsible men near a baby. (And I'm not sure it is wise.) Practically no one makes a salary that could provide enough help to care for five children under six years old today, and even if you could get servants, you should not, our culture says, because "what children need is their fathers."

A very large manufacturing concern in this country, when they were getting ready to prepare men for the next step up in the echelon, called them in and said, "Now this next step you're going to be groomed for is a tough one, and it's going to take sometimes as much as eighteen hours a day. Go home and ask your wives and children if they will let you." True to our picture of American life, they went home, and half of the wives and children vetoed it immediately, so the men didn't make any effort to go on. The family said "No! We like picnics." The company took the group that did go on, and they harried them. They would just let them get home, sit down to dinner, and they'd call them back. Sunday morning the family would just have the picnic all packed, and the telephone would say, "Come back to the plant." That got rid of another 50 per cent. Then they took the few that were left and promoted them.

This is serious. This is a situation in which life in the suburbs—the plumbing, the babies, the azaleas, and the cub scouts—is given precedence over the job of production and distribution which is necessary to this country. One reason that these young people are so unwilling to put as much of an investment in work as their parents did is because they don't believe in the future. The heritage of World War II and then of the Korean conflict coming so soon afterwards has left them with a lack of belief in any kind of predictable long-run future. It's due partly to the atom bomb, partly to the continual statement that we are helpless, that we can't do anything in the world except take part in an armament race, partly to the possibility of military service at any moment.

The result is that people's interests are focused on wanting to live now, and living doesn't mean "making a living." They still want the money, but the general theory is that anybody can make $20,000 with a little luck. The notion that it's *hard* to work, and *hard* to make money is disappearing from young people's image of life.

In concluding this section, we should emphasize individual differences. If most organizations are correct in their assessment of those who apply for jobs, there is hardly a surplus of well-trained individuals with the initiative, risk-taking temperament, and drive that many jobs require. These personality characteristics are scarce. Fortunately, perhaps, as Strauss argues, many jobs don't ask for such traits. In a later section, however, we shall want to question the ability of the organization adequately to select people with these scarce attributes at times when they are necessary and even crucial to job performance.

Professor Eli Ginzberg of the Columbia Graduate School of Business faculty, a noted economist and manpower expert, echoes some of these same observations in the following remarks:

HOW MANY PEOPLE POSSESS A HIGH ORDER OF INITIATIVE?[3]

Basic to the criticism of large organizations is the assumption that initiative is a trait widely distributed throughout the population and

[3] The balance of this chapter is taken from Professor Ginzberg's remarks at the Arden House conference.

that the barriers which society has itself erected, especially in its large organizations, alone prevent its flowering.

A challenge to this assumption is in order. A strong case can be made for the fact that initiative is a scarce trait and that most men are by nature followers not leaders, concerned with playing it safe rather than with struggling to break out on their own. Substantial support for this challenge can be found in the following argument.

The personal exercise of initiative presupposes the existence of:

1. Strong personal goals
2. A substantial degree of physical and emotional energy
3. A willingness to take the risks involved in acting and to accept the consequences of being wrong
4. An ability to deviate from established ways and to tolerate criticism from supervisors and peers about such deviations

HOW MUCH INITIATIVE CAN LARGE ORGANIZATIONS EFFECTIVELY USE?

I am reminded of the directive that the Deputy Chief of Staff of the United States Army, during World War II, addressed to all senior personnel in the Pentagon to reduce the number of reclaimers, stating that the War Department had an Operations Division charged with thinking ahead and making plans and that everybody else should "stop thinking and get on with their work." It is necessary to recognize that despite sincere efforts of business to decentralize, major decisions will inevitably float to the top, where only a relatively few people can participate. The Army knew that major decisions could be made only at the top.

Several years ago one of the country's leading mining companies found itself with three able vice-presidents, all in their early forties, and a president in his early fifties. My informal opinion was asked as to what the company might do to take full advantage of the competence of this able group. My prescription was either to have the president retire or else to encourage one or two of the vice-presidents to move out. From the facts presented, the company's effective use of all four did not appear feasible to me. I was fearful that these able men would spend most of their time jockeying for position.

General Motors has repeatedly prided itself on the fact that it has four men behind every key position. If its claim is valid, it suggests that many men are apparently willing to trade income for opportunities to utilize their full potential.

Another example from the automotive industry is relevant. When a very strong man, like Caruso, is placed as head of a major division (Ford Motor Car Division) his initiative may unbalance the rest of the organization. Balance can frequently be restored only by moving him back into the central group.

The drift of my argument can be formulated thus:

1. Large organizations cannot absorb an indefinite amount of initiative.

2. Much of the strength of large organizations is grounded in traditions, stability of policy, and a vast complex of informal relationships. People with strong initiative are likely to find these forces irksome and inhibiting.

3. Men with strong initiative are likely to possess strong personal goals which usually include the speedy accumulation of power and prestige. Since there are only a limited number of jobs at the top of every organization, some of the men with the most initiative are likely to become impatient waiting for their chance to get ahead and will prefer to move on to other organizations.

4. As I pointed out in an essay some years ago, the coming of age of the large corporation with its split between owners and managers necessitates a reconsideration of the ways in which managers are likely to employ their talents; for it is no longer possible to argue, as had the classical economists, that the efforts of managers will always be directed toward the maximization of profits.

Large corporations are as much, or even more, political entities than economic institutions, and the way to the top requires the skillful exercise of political talents. This means that much of the initiative in large organizations is inevitably channeled into the political game of building strength for oneself and weakening the position of one's present and potential rivals.

By this time the reader may have fallen into the trap of assuming that most large organizations are utopian in their use of human resources. Even without some concern over the employment opportunities for professors interested in problems, not utopias, one would be forced to conclude that a host of challenges face the leaders of contemporary business organizations. We have tried to show that they are not the simplistic ones some critics have found easiest to display. However, they are closely related to them.

Based on some of the most current empirical research in organizational behavior, our conclusion would be that much additional energy needs to be devoted to:

■ Avoiding adverse selection procedures and developing techniques for identifying, attracting, and retaining more outstanding people
■ Finding organizational techniques for taking advantage of the motivation provided by the small group without paying a high price in terms of excessive divisiveness and destructive internal competition
■ Improving the qualities of leadership that mobilize the talents of subordinates

The above are some of the questions which will be dealt with in Part III, the next and concluding section of this volume.

PART III

*Persisting challenges
to large organizations*

chapter **10**

Identifying and rewarding
the talented individual*

Recent research indicates that a surprisingly large number of businesses are failing to identify and develop young managers with the potential for exercising initiative.

Some of these people are casualties of rigid hiring criteria and are lost even before they get on the payroll. Others, having cleared the hiring hurdle, are indoctrinated to the point of intimidation. Some are obscured by overstaffing, which makes recognition of the individual's abilities difficult. Still others are tucked away in unchallenging jobs that either dry up their initiative or make them so dissatisfied that they leave.

The problem of finding men with initiative is serious, because the supply of such people is limited. In the 1960s the number of males in the prime-age working group will dwindle. This means that competition for the most aggressive and talented will be keen and at times ruthless.

The man most organizations are looking for has four characteristics: strong personal goals—he knows where he wants to go; abundant physical and emotional energy; a willingness to take risks—to be dif-

* This chapter is adapted from the article by Prof. Eli Ginzberg which appeared in *Nations Business*, April, 1961, pp. 74ff. In it he developed many of the ideas he presented at the conference.

93

ferent, to take the consequences for decisions, good and bad; and political skill—the ability to influence and manage people.

All companies, whatever their size, need individuals with these dynamic qualities. The currently popular notion that large organizations crush initiative under the sheer weight of size is misleading. The past sixty years have witnessed a rapid expansion of our economy, and in these same years large organizations have grown rapidly. Such growth could not have occurred if size were the natural enemy of initiative.

The fact is that initiative can be encouraged or strangled in any enterprise, depending on the habits of the enterprise. Close study of the following good and bad practices will assist any leader in devising more effective methods for building initiative in an organization:

1. *Hiring practices*

Sometimes hiring practices can keep a company from attracting the kind of people it really wants. The personnel department evolves a stereotype of the young man suitable for the executive ladder—usually a copy of people already in the organization. The standard is poor, because, by definition, an individual with initiative is going to be somewhat different.

Selection and testing methods also offer little comfort for the company searching for men with initiative. The only sure way that business can get something out of somebody is to let him prove himself by actual work. Only by giving a man a job to do can the organization learn who can take risks and who cannot; who has the real energies and who does not; who has strong personal goals and who does not. A man who looks good on paper may look quite different under fire.

2. *Too much indoctrination*

It's true that a person needs some orientation in order to perform reasonably, quickly, and effectively in a new job. But when he is taught the ways of the organization and learns that everything must be done according to established procedure, his capacity and willingness to exercise initiative are shrunk. He becomes leery of bucking the way in which the company's business has usually been transacted.

Initiative means to think up new or improved ways of doing things.

The people who really want to exercise personal initiative in any kind of organization are in the minority. Their scarcity underscores the need for taking pains not to snuff out the spark of initiative.

The best development programs are those in which the management clearly understands the objective. If management doesn't know what it wants to accomplish, the curriculum and the efforts spent in carrying it out tend to be ineffective. The major goal of development programs is to try to broaden the horizons of some of the people who have been caught in routine jobs.

3. Career programs

People should not be hired on a lifetime basis. An organization must keep the way open to correct mistakes.

Some firms tell a young person, "If you perform effectively you can spend your entire working life with us," and then point out that many of the company's benefits are deferred benefits. Pensions do not become the employee's property until late in his career, with many desirable benefits coming only after a man has been with the organization for twenty-five years.

This practice makes it difficult for the organization to correct mistakes in initial hirings. If people are added who have little initiative, the firm is stuck with them as long as they behave and is prevented from hiring someone else.

The fact that a man may get benefits toward the end of his career makes him tend to play it safe, to avoid placing himself in a position where he challenges authority to a point where the organization may have to get him out. Business needs people who are willing to take a stand. A man with his eye on a pension may be unwilling to "stick his neck out." Many companies would be better off if they gave employees title to their benefits much earlier and encouraged people to leave when they have reached their ceiling in the organization. Such employees might be able to make productive careers elsewhere, and the organization would be able to bring in other people to meet its needs.

Happily, there is a trend in this direction. An increasing number of companies are reducing the age at which various benefits are provided. Some companies, facing a profit squeeze, are accelerating retirements. The abrasive part of this policy is that many people look on leaving as a defeat, and deferred benefits make resignation costly. If one could make the costs of leaving less by enabling a man to carry his benefits with him, and if more people began to resign or change jobs, leaving would no longer be equated with defeat.

The Armed Forces let many people out at forty-five, and their leaving inflicts no major stigma. It's well understood that many of these people may have a second career. This goes for other sectors of society as well.

4. *Watching people*

A business must keep an up-to-date inventory of its most capable people and must offer them challenges and problems to test their capacity for exercising initiative.

One of the strengths of large organizations is their ability to practice a high degree of specialization. Their concentration on certain fields means that men will have relatively narrow assignments. It is not easy for a man with initiative to find the scope that he desires in situations where existing policies and procedures outline how the work is to be carried out and where the range of work is somewhat narrowly constricted. Nor is it possible usually for large organizations to move men out of an assignment just as soon or shortly after they have mastered it, although the change would help to keep men's interest alive by facing them with new *learning*.

Companies with decentralized divisions face the danger of losing track of their most competent personnel. Good men get buried in a subsidiary. Unless an active program of personnel control and constant inspection and revaluation are under way, these people may not have opportunities to prove themselves and move up. If they are left behind, their initiative is likely to atrophy. Current research has shown that some able men who formerly worked for large companies have left research posts to set up their own businesses. Their reason? They thought they would have more elbow room, more scope for development than they would have fighting their way through a large hierarchy. Many companies have eight or nine levels of supervision. That many layers can be an obstacle to the identification of people with initiative in the ranks.

If an organization decentralizes, there ought to be a parallel move to build up a strong personnel department in headquarters which has the job of staying aware of the people assigned outside. Staff executives need to be reminded of their responsibility for keeping track of people in line jobs. As they travel in the field, the marketing man at headquarters, the controller, the vice-president should always be on the lookout for bright young people. They should know where potentially promotable people are so that they can tap them when an opportunity arises.

They say the late General George C. Marshall's success as Chief of Staff of the Army in World War II grew out of the fact that he spent crucial years at Fort Benning in the 1930s and, while there, made a careful roster of the performance of all the younger officers who went through.

Later on, he knew whom to call upon when he needed to assemble a strong supporting staff. The story is a good object lesson.

5. *Permitting self-selection*

Management has the responsibility of assigning people tough jobs and letting them tackle the work. The only way a person can grow is to gain self-confidence by knowing that he can master difficult assignments. People get an important psychological lift out of doing a hard job well, a lift which makes them more willing to try the next one. It's essential, therefore, to keep challenging assignments moving out to aggressive young managers and to keep the managers moving on to new assignments when they have mastered the previous ones.

(Compare this with Margaret Mead's observation on p. 85!)

Not all the responsibility rests with management. The individual with initiative will often smoke himself out. His own thrust will move him into a position where he is noticed. Moreover, most people have a fairly realistic view of themselves—and will not overbid.

A pitfall to be avoided is hoarding capable people. Many supervisors will try to hold a competent young fellow in his present job because he has become efficient. Someone else wants to move him ahead. In such instances the long-range good of the organization should always take precedence. If top management keeps an eye on the able and aggressive employee, the dangers of his upward movement being frustrated can be overcome.

An organization with too many people can't promote much expression of initiative, because people will be getting in each other's way and will get lost in the thickets. The tendency to stockpile personnel against future needs costs dearly in two ways: It destroys the potentialities of people who have something in them, because you don't challenge them, and you don't leave enough scope in the organization to stretch good people as far as they can be stretched.

6. Using extra-tough jobs

In any company, extraordinarily difficult but important assignments have to be handled. The job may be opening a branch in a remote and climatically unpleasant area, or a service involving extended travel. When such things come up, management should pay close attention to volunteers. Willingness to volunteer could be an important clue to the man who really has the initiative that will be needed not only for the present but later on.

One of the large chemical companies constantly creates conditions designed to discover the men willing to take on extra work loads; it sometimes pulls men off their regular jobs to see what they can do with tougher assignments. This conscious program of capacity stretching has paid off. More such programs would be useful to business because the problem is really to differentiate between the great mass of people who are perfectly willing to do a good day's work but don't want to do much more and the small minority who have both the prerequisites and the desire to push ahead—who are willing to offer suggestions about change and take the consequences if their suggestions don't pan out.

In large companies, which often break up a job into many parts, the danger is that people will fail to see how their relatively small contribution fits into the whole. Try continually to broaden the job of the individual. This policy, called work enlargement, is a valuable tool. Through its use you may help a man to avoid the stultification which sets in if he feels he is trapped.

7. Evaluating a performance

A major problem that every organization faces is how to evaluate the work that people do. The problem is made more complex by the fact that much of their work is done not as individuals but as members of a team or group.

Most people in middle management are there because they have failed to get to the top or are still trying to advance. Hence they are not likely to assess sympathetically younger people who demonstrate strong initiative and who are evidently potential competitors.

When organizations are not able to establish an objective system of executive evaluation, most ambitious men will try to operate in a manner that does not bring them into conflict with their superiors, whose subjective evaluations of them will largely determine their future.

Can more critical and correct readings on the actual performance of individuals be made?

At a minimum, multiple readings on an individual should be obtained. Relying on an appraisal made by one man means a high risk of getting a biased evaluation. Two or three people, independent of a man's immediate superior, should be asked to give reports.

Not all evaluations have to be made solely in terms of the individual. One can evaluate how well the group as a whole performs and in that way learn something about the role of the individual in the group, especially if the man being appraised is the leader. For instance, if a business has several companies or divisions, one can take readings by comparing one with the other on the assumption that if the original distribution of personnel was about the same, differences are due to the leadership.

One of the tough problems in evaluation is that the criteria used to appraise current performance are not always the only important criteria. Some of the contributions that people make may only show up later in the company's development. For instance, in evaluating people in a research laboratory, the appraiser should give a man credit for what he has contributed to this year's productivity or new products; but he should also note that the man working alongside the researcher may have broken open a new area that will take two or three years for the company to exploit. He must have the long-range as well as the short-range perspective.

Top management will accomplish nothing by saying that it is interested in having a lot of personal initiative shown, if it then follows a dull and dreary method of promotion or distribution of bonuses which fails to reinforce what management says. You can't talk one way and act another and have good staff morale.

8. *Keeping the ranks thin*

Organizations should be kept lean. People should be given more work than they can handle, because a certain amount of pressure means that the less important work will drop by the side. In the present period, with a profit squeeze which is likely to continue, top management would be well advised to consider ways of thinning out its ranks. Eliminating superfluous personnel is the best way to create and to maintain an environment in which good people come through fast. But don't go too far; when the howls about the work load become genuine, it's time to stop.

Another technique which business should consider is setting aside the formalities of rank in certain instances to achieve more effective performance and the proper exercise of initiative. For example, a particular problem may at a certain time require the leadership of a man in a subordinate capacity who has greater technical knowledge of the problem than his superior has. There is no reason, on a short-run basis, why the subordinate and superior shouldn't temporarily exchange places. In the scientific field in general, and particularly in university-directed projects, this exchange is made quite freely. Business could profitably imitate the technique.

Professor Ginzberg has raised many stimulating questions concerning the efficacy of some current selection and placement techniques. More important, he has proposed greater reliance on direct methods of observation, on encouraging self-selection, and, in general, on finding out about the individual by systematic evaluation of his behavior under the stresses and strains of organization life.

Recently, Dr. Eliot Chapple and I also tried to summarize our criticisms of some of the uses of psychological testing in industry.[1] Just one excerpt from that paper may provide an appropriate conclusion for this chapter:

It is a curious commentary on our highly pragmatic business society that most attempts to appraise the personalities of people who make organiza-

---

[1] There has been a growing number of complaints about misuses, misinterpretations, and irresponsibilities associated with the use of testing procedures. Cf. Martin L. Gross, *The Brain Watchers*, Random House, Inc., New York, 1962.

tions work are mystical and introspective. In everyday life, we recognize that what people actually do is the significant thing and tell our children that "actions speak louder than words." Yet, research effort has concentrated on finding out something about the person's interior life through the use of ink blots, pictures, questionnaires, or the full-fledged treatment on the psycho-analyst's couch. That which is learned from the resulting word patterns is highly difficult even for the experts to interpret. Too often their findings remind one of the sacred oracle at Delphi repeating the message of the gods in words so tangential to meaning that only the fact can prove the soothsayer right.

The dilemma everyone faces, of course, derives from concentrating on the internal goings-on of the individual. Everyone realizes how hard it is even to understand the significance of one's own reactions, but with these methods the executive is forced to jump from the unknown (or very tenuously known) to the actual behavior of other persons. Great novelists may successfully probe the inner workings of the human personality; such freedom of creation is not at hand for the manager.

Regardless of what technique is used, any theories about an individual can be substantiated only by what he does, that is, by his behavior in specific situations. No matter what words are used to describe his personality and temperament, they have meaning only if they help predict his actual behavior. We grant, of course, that tests may provide other interesting and useful information; but from the managerial point of view, such information is often irrelevant to the organization. It may be fascinating to know an executive is "orally dependent," "ego inadequate," or, more traditionally, "moderately introverted," but the manager needs only to know how his state of mind will affect his actions in the company.

The desire to learn what makes another person act as he does also raises serious ethical questions. There is increasing resistance to an employer or prospective employer probing into the personal and private areas of an employee's mind. In spite of the assurances of the testers, information concerning mental health, much of which may be neither valid nor relevant, is often circulated within the organization. The result is more than an unnecessary gratification of curiosity; it is also a serious invasion of privacy, breaking down the division between the world of work and the world of private life. The authors seriously question the right of an employer to seek or know such information, even in the garbled form in which he usually comprehends it.

Actually, the terms and concepts used frequently fail to help the administrator identify the kind of performance to expect of the individual. Although they provide some notion of his overall potentiality, anyone who has appraised employee performance knows how difficult it is to prove such predictions right or wrong. The persons for whom such tests are given usually hold jobs that do not permit easy assessment of output and productivity.[2]

[2] Eliot D. Chapple and Leonard R. Sayles, *The Measure of Management,* The Macmillan Company, New York, 1961, pp. 114–115.

chapter 11

Physical health, mental health, and the corporate environment *

When the original materials for this symposium were being assembled, we were fortunate in having the assistance of a physician, an internist who has devoted a good deal of his professional expertise to studying the health of people in large organizations. We were interested in his observations because they seemed to highlight a growing problem: the tendency for organizations to use selection procedures to exclude the more troublesome, critical, or even less healthy employee in favor of the more placid, passive individual. Dr. Lawrence E. Hinkle's findings cast real doubts on the usual, easy assumption that better employees are those who are easiest to deal with and who get along best with everyone around them. (They also raise some serious questions concerning the growing efforts to "sensitize" people to their own failings so that they will be more likely to develop friendly relationships.)

Another interesting aspect of the work of Dr. Hinkle and of Cornell University Medical College's Human Ecology study program is to point out the importance of the relationship of the organization to the

* The major portion of this chapter is by Dr. Lawrence E. Hinkle, Jr., of the Department of Medicine, New York Hospital, Cornell Medical Center.

larger society and the impossibility of comprehending the "inside" without looking at the "outside." [1]

It has been found that, in any group of similar people living and working in the same environment, some members have had a great deal more illness than others. The explanation for this susceptibility lies not so much in the characteristics of the environment as in the characteristics of the people. By and large, the agents responsible for illness are widely and randomly distributed throughout any environment. Most of the viral, bacterial, and allergenic agents thought to be responsible for the acute respiratory and gastrointestinal illnesses, many of the po-

---

[1] Over the past ten years, the Human Ecology study program at Cornell University Medical College has made an intensive investigation of the lifetime health patterns of more than 3,000 people from seven population groups, and of the way that their experiences with their jobs, their families, the people around them, and the societies in which they live have influenced their susceptibility to illness. Among those studied are several groups of people from various levels of large American corporations. They have included a group of semiskilled working-women, a group of skilled craftsmen, a group of foremen and supervisors recently promoted to management positions and now making their way up the corporate ladder, another group of young college graduates recently appointed to junior managerial positions and also making their way up the corporate ladder, and executives at all levels up to that of vice-president. The studies have been carried out by investigators from the fields of medicine, psychiatry, psychology and sociology—and on some occasions with the help of a cultural anthropologist. For some related research, see:

1. Lawrence E. Hinkle, Jr. and Norman Plummer, "Life Stress and Industrial Absenteeism: The Concentration of Illness in One Segment of a Working Population," *Industrial Medicine and Surgery*, vol. 21, p. 363, 1952.
2. Lawrence E. Hinkle, Jr. and Harold G. Wolff, "Health and the Social Environment: Experimental Investigations," chap. 4 in A. H. Leighton, J. A. Clausen, and R. N. Wilson (eds.), *Explorations in Social Psychiatry*, Basic Books, Inc., Publishers, New York, 1957.
3. Lawrence E. Hinkle, Jr., "Physical Health, Mental Health, and the Social Environment: Some Characteristics of Healthy and Unhealthy People," chap. 4 in Ralph H. Ojemann (ed.), *Recent Contributions of Biological and Psychosocial Investigations to Preventive Psychiatry*, State University of Iowa, Iowa City, Iowa, 1959.
4. William N. Christenson and Lawrence E. Hinkle, Jr., "Differences in Illness and Prognostic Signs in Two Groups of Young Men," *Journal of the American Medical Association*, vol. 177, p. 247, 1961.
5. Lawrence E. Hinkle, Jr., Norman Plummer, and L. H. Whitney, "The Continuity of Patterns of Illness and the Prediction of Future Health," *Journal of Occupational Medicine*, vol. 3, p. 417, 1961.

tential sources of trauma responsible for minor injuries, and a great many of the various types of interpersonal relations and life situations thought to be implicated in the so-called "functional" disorders, are in this category. Illnesses caused by such agents are responsible for the greater amount of short-term sickness disability. Furthermore, the various toxic, dietary, mechanical, and hereditary factors which are concerned with the chronic degenerative, metabolic, and neoplastic diseases, and which are responsible for the major proportion of premature disability and retirement, are also widely distributed. Thus, in any working environment, the potential causes of disease are widespread; yet most of the time only a few people become ill. One finds that the greater proportion of sickness in any given group of people is concentrated in a relatively small proportion of its members, who not only have a greater number of illnesses but also have a greater variety of illnesses.

One might add that, on the whole, these more frequently ill people whom we have observed have had a disproportionate number of disturbances of mood, thought, and behavior, and partly for this reason, they have created additional problems by their attitudes toward their work and their relations with other people. Yet these people were not qualitatively different from the others in their group. Twenty-five per cent of the people accounted for 50 per cent of the illness simply because illness seemed to be distributed in this way among the general population of adults. One might equally well have said that 10 per cent of the population accounted for 25 per cent of the illness, or that 50 per cent accounted for 75 per cent of the illness. In making such a statement one is merely pointing out an epidemiological phenomenon which has important consequences.

We were unable to locate any individual in any population who was utterly without illness for any length of time. As I have indicated, many evidences supported the conclusion that genetic inheritance is one of the major determinants of health patterns. But I should rather comment on our observations of the social and psychological characteristics of "healthy" and "unhealthy" people.

We have found both healthy and unhealthy people at every level of every society that we have studied. Very healthy people have been found among the lowest marginal and least privileged members of our own society. Monetary income itself, above a subsistence level, does not seem to be an important determinant of health. Good health can be present despite severe economic and social deprivation and despite the experience of profound culture change and social dislocation. However, in our experience, deprivation and social dislocation were often associated with ill health. Mobility within one's own society, either upward or downward, was quite often associated with ill health.

Very healthy people, in general, were inclined to conform to the requirements of the particular niche in the particular society in which they lived. Many, though not all, of the unhealthy were nonconformists. In terms of the values of the segment of society from which they came —that is to say, in the attainment of honors, titles, and material possessions—we found very little difference between the very healthy and the unhealthy. In fact, except where the possession of good health was a prerequisite for attainment, the achievements of the unhealthy, it seems to us, were likely to exceed those of the very healthy.

In the groups that we have studied, the unhealthy people were somewhat more likely to be productive, creative, or otherwise outstanding people than were the very healthy. However, the most productive and creative people did not fall into either end of the distribution curve but usually stood near the middle. Poor health was no touchstone of success, and it was often crippling.

The most healthy people were often described as likable, unobtrusive, reliable people, who were accepted but rarely admired. Though almost never disliked or hated, they were seldom emulated. The unhealthy, by contrast, were often described as annoying, disturbing, unreliable people, who were frequently rejected, often disliked and hated, but were sometimes admired and emulated.

The healthy were likely to have grown up in a stable and cohesive family with good and protective interpersonal relations; but sometimes, as has been seen, they originated in broken families where they experienced turmoil of various kinds. About half of the unhealthy people we have seen have grown up in an atmosphere of conflict, rejection, deprivation, and illness; but the other half originated from "good" backgrounds.

In adult life the very healthy usually exist in an environment, whatever it may be, in which their relation to their group, to their marriage partners, and to their occupations is bilaterally satisfactory. But sometimes one sees healthy people for whom one, or even two, of these relationships may be unsatisfactory. I do not think I have ever seen a healthy person for whom all these relationships were unsatisfactory. Usually when we found that a man's job and his relation to his group were not good, we found a conspicuously strong relationship to his family, or vice versa.

The unhealthy usually existed in an adult environment in which two or three of these relationships were conspicuously poor; but sometimes unhealthy people existed in an adult environment in which these relationships were "good."

The healthiest people that we have seen sometimes had purely personal or selfish goals, concerned with their own comfort and security. About half of those whom we have studied have shown conspicuous lack of emotional involvement with other people. They were described as isolated, insulated people who "don't let things bother them." A great many of them behaved as if they felt no deep responsibility for the welfare of other people. In general, they behaved as if they were quite content with their lot in life, whatever it might have been. About 70 per cent of them had been conspicuously without "ambition," as we view this trait in our society. Four-fifths, approximately, had seen their occupations as "satisfactory," their marriages as "good," and their life situations as interesting, satisfying, and rewarding. Inwardly, we found them placid, certain, self-satisfied, without conflict, and with few doubts.

The least healthy people we often found to be people who were outwardly directed, with socially determined goals—people who desired to improve their status, to get ahead, to "be a good son," to "become a teacher," to "do something creative," to "fight for a better social system," and so on. Some 80 per cent of them had been people with great emotional involvement with other people; love, hate, compassion, sympathy, liking, and disliking were features of their lives. They were described by others as sensitive, feeling people. Often they behaved as if they were entirely responsible for the welfare of others, for whom they may not necessarily have had any direct responsibility. Among them we have seen people who supported aged parents, cared for sick relatives, educated children, tried to do the job right, or "fought on to the last,"—often at the expense of their own welfare. The majority of them have behaved as if they were utterly discontented with their lot in life and would have liked it to be very different. They were often described as ambitious people. They were inclined to regard their lives as dull, frustrating, and hateful, and their marriages as painful, unpleasant, confining, and demanding. They looked on life in general as frustrating, threatening, demanding, challenging, and insecure. Inwardly one found them to be disturbed, uncertain, self-condemning, full of conflict and doubt—often discontented, bitter, anxious, discouraged, and brooding or ruminating.

Our general conclusions were these: Very healthy people—that is, people who had few or no evidences of bodily illness or of disturbances of mood, thought, and behavior, and whose general attitudes, outlook, and behavior conformed to the norms of the social groups of which they were members—usually were people who were peculiarly well fitted for the particular ecological niche in which they found themselves, although they might be peculiarly ill fitted for some other niche. One cannot, therefore, draw specifications for a generally healthy person without specifying his age, sex, cultural and social background, and many facets of his immediate situation in life. The world apparently has room for many types of people—all healthy.

A good state of health was not necessarily associated with other characteristics that were socially valuable. Specifically, healthy people were not necessarily more creative, productive, responsible, respected, successful, compassionate, honored, or emulated than other comparable and less healthy people in their own social group. Sometimes the personality characteristics of healthy people and the social value placed on their behavior made them less attractive than people who were less healthy.

Freedom from illness or maximal health, therefore, must be looked upon as only one measure of the adaptation of the individual to his environment. It is not always the best measure of this adaptation. The unhealthy do not necessarily do less well than the healthy in other areas of life. Sometimes ill health or even death is the price of superior performance as a human being.

Some of these observations seem to have a special pertinence to life in a corporate organization. The industrial organizations that we have studied have tended to attract to them, at every level of the organization, people of similar ethnic and social background. To a large extent conformity among the group has not been imposed by the company, but has been an outgrowth of the relationship of the corporate organization to the society in which it exists. Men and women within a corporate organization, therefore, experience pressures for conformity to certain norms of attitude and behavior, not simply from the organization itself but also from the group of which they are a part, and the latter pressure is often more important than the former. Our investigations of men in management capacities have indicated that those who start up the management ladder from an upper-middle-class background and a college education experience far fewer threats, challenges, and demands than those who begin the climb from a working-class background and with a high school education. The difficulties of the high school men arise not so much from the actual challenges of the job as from the much more pervading challenges of moving from one social category to another. In comparing two similar groups of such men, we found that the high school men have experienced significantly more domestic, financial, and interpersonal difficulties, and find significantly more demands upon their time, arising from their need to acquire more education and training at night, and to acquire other characteristic that go with their new status in life. These men, often of superior drive and ability, nevertheless have experienced a good deal more illness per unit time than their running mates, who have not had to make so many adaptations.

The requirements of an industrial organization sometimes place conflicting demands upon the individuals within it. At any level within an organization, value is placed upon people who are happily adjusted to their jobs and to those around them, who work steadily and effectively, who create few administrative problems, and who are well satisfied with their lot in life and with the organization for which they work. In our experience, such people are quite likely to be healthy and well liked, and often because of these characteristics, they are promoted. One also finds, however, that the very characteristics which cause them to be of so much value carry with them parallel and self-defeating detriments. In many instances such people lack the discontent, the drive, and the ambition necessary to impel them to seek new challenges, and often they are inclined to avoid such challenges, if they can do so. The most ambitious, driving, and able people are not infrequently dissatisfied and forceful, and have difficulty in getting along with those around them. Usually they are not the healthiest members of the group; often they are disliked by their associates; and sometimes they create administrative problems. Often this maladjustment prevents them from obtaining the advancement they so desire and at the same time deprives the corporation of the services of a person who might do well in new and more responsible capacities. The man who becomes a successful executive, therefore, may not be a man who has all the characteristics which would make him a valuable and successful employee at another level within the organization. It appears to us that these conflicting social demands, which are somewhat inherent in the nature of the corporate organization, go a long way toward explaining why many people who have been successful at lower levels fail to do well at higher levels and may even try to avoid advancement, whereas others who seem to have superior abilities sometimes fail to obtain the advancement which they so avidly desire, and may become problems to the organization because of their thwarted ambitions.

chapter **12**

When the psychiatrist
may not help

The two preceding chapters have challenged many easy assumptions about finding the "right type" of person for a position of responsibility in the large organization. There has been a tendency to assume that a simple, positive correlation exists between "well-adjusted" people (i.e., as identified by psychological testing) and job performance. Not only is this assumption shown to be fallacious, but so is the parallel belief that an employee's or a manager's behavior can be predicted independently of a careful analysis of the requirements of his job and the pressures these generate for him.

Industry is often faced with the problem of dealing with the disturbed employee *after* selection and placement decisions have been made. Dr. Eliot Chapple, an anthropologist and longtime researcher and consultant in industry, has criticized the tendency of psychiatrists practicing in industry to neglect techniques by which organizational and personality variables can both be dealt with. Chapple's findings, like those of Ginzberg and Hinkle, encourage greater reliance on close observation of individuals' reactions to specific jobs rather than on grander generalizations about correct and incorrect personality types.*

* The major portion of Dr. Chapple's material is taken from his article "Contributions of Anthropology to Institutional Psychiatry," *Human Organization*, vol. 13, no. 2, pp. 11–13, Summer, 1954. Certain additions and deletions have been made for the purpose of this chapter.

LIMITATIONS OF PSYCHIATRY
IN ORGANIZATIONAL SITUATIONS

Psychiatry in its present stage of development is often unable to come to grips with the effects of organizational life on mental health.[1] As a result of the almost all-pervasive influence of the psychoanalysts, the tendency is to place major emphasis on the predisposing effects of early childhood on the personality and to ignore the way specific organizational situations, in the family or on the job, predispose or precipitate an illness. Consequently, except where psychiatric practice is concerned with the immediate alleviation of severe symptoms, the consultant assumes that the only really adequate solution of the personal problem is to "remake" the personality, trying to eliminate or substantially modify the effects of early childhood. From the business point of view, psychiatry's conceptual framework provides no method which can be used in an organization to spot individuals who are (or more important, who can become) vulnerable to specific types of stress, or any means of defining what constitutes a stress and how to determine its effects on a given individual.

People are referred to the psychiatrist by immediate supervisors or through staff departments, particularly by those concerned with personnel and health; hence referrals depend upon the sophistication of managers in the organization, and, in spite of the use of films and much educational effort, they are almost universally naïve where adults are concerned. Even if organizations say that in principle they believe in giving a psychiatric examination together with a physical, actually very few of them give a thorough physical examination to all employees, even on initial employment. Moreover, such examinations would need to be repeated at least annually, and though management might be convinced that periodic retesting was the only answer to its problems, the practical difficulties of conducting the examinations, as well as the expense, would be almost prohibitive.

The fact is, the present orientation of much psychiatry makes its use

[1] Doctors Hinkle and Wolff of Cornell University Medical College in New York report that "physiological changes associated with attempts to adapt to environmental situations influenced the time of occurrence of all types of diseases, had an effect upon the health patterns of two-thirds of these adults, and were involved in the development of at least one-third of all illnesses experienced by" a series of more than 3,000 persons.

by the organization random and wasteful, particularly in the crucial matter of case finding. Having no way of dealing with the disease-producing aspects of organizational situations, and being without a means of evaluating on a routine basis the propensities of any given individual to succumb to stress, the psychiatrist can hope to do little more than try to raise the level of awareness of the members of the organization as to the signs and symptoms of psychiatric (emotional) disorders; he can only hope for enough time to screen out cases from the large number of leads that such a program might turn up. Moreover, most present psychotherapeutic methods, being unrelated to the conditioning effects of the organization and incapable of using them as part of the treatment, are too time-consuming for practical purposes.

The key to the problem lies in the conception of case finding as it is defined in public health. Without a theory and a method to determine the points where the disease may be expected to appear, the psychiatrist is operating as much in the dark as would the specialist in contagious diseases, if he had no knowledge of the way malaria or bubonic plague is transmitted and of the factors conditioning the rate of spread of the disease. It may be true that modern chemistry will at long last develop a true cure for malaria, but the knowledge of the part played by the mosquito, and by particular species of mosquitoes under specific environmental conditions, provides a much more effective and practical means of wiping out the disease than treatment of individual illnesses. It is in this broad conception of case finding, which depends upon a thorough understanding of the causes of the various psychiatric disorders and of the environmental factors which affect their management in psychotherapy, that our present point of view can be of value.

Extensive studies in the field of business and industry have shown that the individual's performance and his degree of adjustment or maladjustment (as it is made immediately evident psychiatrically or "psychosomatically" in the production of symptoms) are directly related to how well his personality and temperament fit the particular position in the organizational network—as it is constituted by other personalities and constrained by a specific cultural framework. Experiments have demonstrated repeatedly that transfers from an organizational position for which the personality is not fitted, to the proper one, create major changes in mood and performance; conversely, experiments have also shown the harmful effects on an individual of his transfer to a job involving stress, even though the transfer may give him a promotion and substantial advantages in terms of recognition and salary. Too often organizations reap the results of hasty placement decisions; an effective human being placed in a job for which he is unfitted develops ulcers or high blood pressure, or gets a coronary.

Dr. George Strauss has completed an excellent case study of the effects on a group of skilled mechanics (set-up men) of major organizational changes.[2] In this manufacturing company, a series of changes were introduced which radically transformed the men's jobs. These involved changes in the number and types of personalities to whom they reported and with whom they worked; the range of contacts they enjoyed with subordinates; and the frequency with which certain production crises occurred. Strauss reports that during the ensuing twelve-month period, seven of the total of twelve set-up men became ill. While absolute proof is lacking, a large share of these problems would normally be associated with psychiatric disturbances.

■ Set-up man A: Died of heart attack. Everyone said the attack was due to overwork.
■ Set-up man B: Nervous twitches became substantially more serious; caused himself a painful back injury, for which he was hospitalized.
■ Set-up man C: Constant complaints of stomach pains; taken to hospital reportedly for an emergency appendicitis operation; after three days of observation, no organic faults detected.
■ Set-up man D: Nervous breakdown; on advice of doctor, left plant to work as bartender.
■ Set-up man E: Stomach condition.
■ Set-up man F: Sick for various reasons twenty-three days in rush-season quarter.
■ Set-up man G: Hernia, out thirty-four days.

Changes in organization, on the other hand, can equally well transform the situation so that persons otherwise suited by personality once again become capable of effective and contented performance. In a number of instances, highly disturbed individuals who, superficially at least, would have been referred to a psychiatrist, have completely lost all signs of pathological behavior and autonomic symptoms, once the source of stress has been removed by changes in the organizational

[2] George Strauss, "The Set-up Man: A Case Study of Organizational Change," *Human Organization,* vol. 13, no. 2, p. 23, 1954.

structure.[3] Such findings are not particularly novel. Their importance lies in the fact that the nature of the stress is highly specific, and that the same or a similar job can be made seriously disturbing or eminently satisfactory with what might appear to be minor changes in the work pattern required of the individual.

PERSONALITY AND TEMPERAMENT FACTORS IN ORGANIZATIONS

Furthermore, in studying people in business organizations, we must emphasize the fact that the kind of pathological behavior that creates serious difficulties is seldom of the type encountered in psychiatric clinics and hospitals. The incidence of psychotic states, or of what might perhaps be called prepsychotic states, is extremely low. Furthermore, though substantially higher in incidence than psychosis, clearly defined patterns of psychoneurosis and disorders familiar in the clinic are far less common and significant than types of pathological behavior classified by psychiatrists as psychopathological or, better still, as "pathological emotionality"—in ordinary parlance, manifestations of temperament. In other words, though people throw the term *neurotic* around to cover every instance of emotional reactions—so that in some circles it becomes the fashion to refer to oneself as neurotic—what they are talking about is not the psychiatrist's definition of the term, i.e., a clear-cut behavioral entity.

We do find people whose primary characteristic might be called "reactability," in contrast to the restricted and rigid patterns of behavior of the neurotic. When such people encounter stress, they underreact or overreact in ways which in psychiatry are loosely called "infantile" (meaning simply that they are most obvious in children). After being dominated, they may become sulky and try to avoid further contacts, or else they may try to talk themselves out of the fancied threat by spinning yarns which in the extreme might be called pathological lies. They are shy and reserved, or, on the contrary, apparently are so concerned

[3] In a three-volume study with the overall title, *The Ineffective Soldier* (Columbia University Press, New York, 1959), our colleague Prof. Eli Ginzberg, concludes after a great deal of research that many soldiers who were rejected from the armed services on psychiatric grounds could have functioned quite satisfactorily in jobs which did not involve certain strains and pressures beyond their limits of endurance.

with making a good impression that they cannot stop talking. They become impatient or "blow up" when they do not get a response.

TEMPERAMENT CHARACTERISTICS IN DIFFERENT ORGANIZATIONS

Apart from such reactive people, we of course also find the individual who is simply misplaced, whose personality is extreme only in comparison with the kinds of people and situations found within a particular organization and who, in another context, would be quite at home and well adjusted. Moreover, a process of natural selection takes place among people employed in business, both as to personality characteristics and as to special kinds of temperamental factors which seem to be related to particular types of jobs and the requirements they make for interaction among the people.

For example, the kinds of personalities found in a department store are very different from those in a government bureau or in an engineering or manufacturing firm. We should expect some such difference in salespeople, regardless of varying conditions in the organization. Yet the need for a fast pace and for high initiative, which extends to all types of jobs in a store, definitely differentiates them from jobs in other types of organizations. For example, in a random sample of 260 department-store employees, slightly over 30 per cent showed a significant occurrence of "persistence," whereas in 500 individuals selected at random in a government agency, significant degrees of this trait were found in only 5 per cent of the sample. In the same way, only 7½ per cent of the sample of 500 people in a government agency showed an indication of a type of emotional reaction which, when extreme, leads to uncontrolled, long-lasting outbursts, while 23 per cent of department-store employees showed this characteristic. We might expect that people in department stores, by the nature of their work, would be more "temperamental." With regard to specific traits, the facts clearly warrant our expectation.

SIGNIFICANT MENTAL HEALTH PROBLEMS IN ORGANIZATIONS

Findings such as these show that the types of cases the psychiatrist is accustomed to handling in the clinic are relatively unimportant in organizations. Of course a significant number of neurotics and mild psychotics do occasionally appear, and they must be recognized and dealt with immediately. Yet the personality problems which turn out to be of major importance in affecting the operations of an organization and the health of the individual are those patterns of reaction in interpersonal relations (in psychiatric terms, the psychopathological) with which very little has been done in psychiatry. In child psychiatry, attention is often paid to these behavioral disturbances, but in the adult they are either loosely classified as neurotic, or regarded as "normal" weaknesses or, in some special cases, as reasons for exclusion from employment.

Moreover, we know very little about the precise relationship of each of these temperamental reactions to the vast group of diseases developed or made worse by stress. We only know generally that "emotional reactions," *not which ones*, are responsible. Some of the most interesting work in this area has been done in cardiology by Doctors Rosenman and Friedman in San Francisco. They have shown that the major factors contributing to the development of coronary disease are affected by specific stresses in the jobs of individuals. Accountants, working to complete an audit or close the books, showed significant increases in measurements of these various factors, which dropped off to more normal levels when the deadline had been reached. Not only was this variation characteristic of the effects of the work situation, but as these investigators have also shown, individuals with specific behavioral patterns have both higher levels of such potentially causative factors as serum cholesterol, blood-clotting rate, and the like, and also a higher incidence of actual coronary artery disease.[4]

Careful placement can go far in dealing with these problems. The determination of the degree of stress the individual can take and the consideration of stress in evaluating job opportunities can play a useful part in adjusting people more effectively to their working environment. We must recognize, nevertheless, that the process of organiza-

[4] R. H. Rosenman and M. Friedman, "The Possible Relationship of Occupational Stress to Clinical Coronary Heart Disease," *California Medicine*, vol. 89, pp. 169–174, September, 1958; M. Friedman, R. H. Rosenman, and V. Carroll, "Changes in the Serum Cholesterol and Blood-clotting Time in Men Subjected to Cyclic Variation of Occupational Stress," *Circulation*, vol. 17, no. 5, May, 1958; M. Friedman and R. H. Rosenman, "Association of Specific Overt Behavior Pattern with Blood and Cardiovascular Findings," *Journal of the American Medical Association*, vol. 169, pp. 1286–1296, Mar. 21, 1959.

tional realignment and the placement of individuals according to their capacities cannot accomplish everything. Men and women will still be affected strongly by the impact of their relationships in other systems, notably in the family. Psychiatrists and other specialists will need increasingly to take into consideration systematically, both in the development (etiology) of the illness and in the management of the therapy, the interdependence of all the organizations in which an individual acts.[5]

If analysis of the situation reveals that the individual's personality has definite vulnerabilities in the jobs in which he finds himself, management should determine whether there are other positions in the organizations in which he can make a better adjustment, whether some kind of individualized program (not necessarily "treatment") is indicated to help him accommodate himself better to his position, or whether training or treatment should be combined with transfer so that the effects of the job and the supportive help of the psychiatrist or personnel specialist will make for a successful shift.

In other words, we view psychiatry as something which cannot be practiced, in corporations at least, independently of the process of measuring the individual's personality and temperament traits and coincidentally measuring the stresses of the job. The organizational situation is, therefore, decisive. It provides the environment which sets emotional disturbance in motion in vulnerable individuals; it must also provide the administrative means by which such disturbances can be corrected or alleviated. Psychiatry and the psychiatrist, however useful, cannot, singlehanded, take over the responsibility or provide the techniques for analysis and decision which must be made by the organization.

[5] See Eliot D. Chapple, "Deliberate Use of Occupational Therapy to Rebuild Human Relations," *Bulletin of the Massachusetts Occupational Therapy Association*, vol. 13, no. 8, pp. 1–6, 1940.

chapter 13

The use and misuse of creative people and ideas*

The modern organization is somewhat unique in endeavoring to build change into its structure and operation. By "build in" we mean the acquisition of people and the creation of departments which are supposed to identify problems with present methods and products and seek improvements. The organization wants to encourage creativity and innovation and to go beyond the perfection of routine, although, as we have argued, this routine is not so easy to attain as the outsider might imagine.

Wilbert Moore was among the first of our distinguished sociologists in the United States to become concerned with the position of the expert, the "staff" person, as he is sometimes called, in the large business organization. Harlan Cleveland has already pointed to the increasing proportion of these experts in the large organization and the opportunities such positions provide for individual initiative. But, as Moore's analysis will suggest, there is ample opportunity for slippage between the giving of the assignment to an individual or a group and its accomplishment within the conservatism of the large organization. When we have seen Dr. Moore's position, we shall turn to a series of case studies that seek to explore in depth the problems he raises.

* This chapter is from materials prepared by Prof. Wilbert Moore for the program. More recently, he has expanded these ideas in a new book, *The Conduct of the Corporation*, Random House, Inc., New York, 1962.

Critics of the corporation say or imply that individual initiative is declining in the face of a "social ethic" of excessive conformity. Nostalgic retrospect often leads to historical distortion, and this slant makes the alleged decline doubtful. (The best single reply to the complaint that "things aren't as they used to be" is, "They never were.") Yet there is certainly contemporary evidence of cultivated collectivism. The metaphors of the team or the family, neither of which the corporation strongly resembles, are widely employed. However, this semantic nonsense appears to be a response to the tremendous and only barely contained heterogeneity and diverse forces in the corporation, rather than an attempt truly to suppress the individual.

In any event, a sociologist can scarcely accept the formula of individual *versus* group. *Purely* individual initiative is both rare and unlikely to be judged constructive. The questions are rather: (1) Which other individuals or groups does our potential creator take as the object of his loyalty, the source of approval, and the legitimate source of restraint on his manic enthusiasms and his depressive tendencies to lethargy? (2) Do these "significant others" encourage and reward initiative? As organized entities, large business enterprises will probably not be accorded such trust, but they may well permit a man's personal identification with functional units, aggregates of occupational peers, and administrative superiors who are accorded legitimacy as well as power.

We should not leave the question of the general supply of creativity without mentioning one additional aspect of motivation. Creativity, although rarely self-rewarding without external confirmation, is self-regenerating. We know, clinically, that nothing fails like failure, and strong evidence supports the aphorism that nothing succeeds like success. The implication of this spiral effect may be seen in two contexts. First, the individual who is frustrated at work is quite unlikely, despite homespun psychological theory, to exemplify his talents elsewhere. Second, the individual accorded recognition for creative achievement at work is likely both to participate more actively in his other roles and to undertake to build upon his recognized record in his work.

The discussion so far has been concerned with the universal or distributive aspects of creativity. The implications for organizational theory and practice will be traced in the following section. First, however, we may consider the situation of those whose positions are commonly thought to require or foster creativity. The qualification "commonly thought" is in fact rather restrictive, for the innovative roles usually identified exclude not only all production and clerical workers but all supervisors and managers below policy-forming executive levels. Indeed, a case can often be made for excluding executives, since they exercise balanced judgment of proposed innovations, with vetoes of improper or untimely ones and implementation of acceptable ones, but often do not initiate change on their own account.

Despite the seeming conservatism bred by success, business enterprises notably devote considerable resources to fostering innovations. (These resources are of course allocated by executive decision.) Innovation is both organized and institutionalized, and therefore not primarily accidental, external, and deplorable. To an increasing extent, for reasons of technical specialization that are well known, innovation is in the first instance a staff function and not in any ordinary sense an executive or entrepreneurial one. This specialization, however, heightens the universal tension between information suppliers and decision makers, that is, thinkers and doers, or in administrative language, staff and line.

Suggestion innovations face the veto powers of administrative superiors, exercised on grounds that are probably unpersuasive to the proposers. If accepted, the innovations are not thereby assured a smooth course. Implementation is a task of lesser administrators, who cannot exercise official vetoes or even persuasive arguments if they are not consulted. Their power is that of sabotage, and their incentives for reluctance will be proportional to the nuisance of the change and their resentment for the failure to draw upon their "long practical experience."

We come, then, to one of the critical problems of creative innovation in the large enterprise, and that is the disproportion between the economic and bureaucratic capacity to take risks and implement change. Large organizations may very well have superior capacity to foster ideas and even to harbor distinctly odd personalities, but they have also a rather severely limited capacity to translate ideas into action because of the many hurdles on the paths of progress. And producers of ideas dismissed as impractical may be more frustrated than those not encouraged to think in the first place.

THE USE OF CREATIVITY

No simple formula will determine when initiative and creativity are constructive and when they are tangential or irrelevant or definitely destructive. A purely static (and wholly unrealistic) model of an organization in a benign environment ideally planned and ideally staffed with participants perfectly motivated leaves no room for constructive change. (It also leaves no necessity for managers.) The appropriate occasions for creativity thus can be identified as the development of the best relationship between the organization and its environing setting, the sharpening and modifying of organizational objectives, and the improvement of the means for achieving them. In effect, easy means of achievement unlocks many doors, if it does not open them. If, within limits, the virtue of creativity is to be encouraged in the setting of the complex organization, it can reliably occur only by deliberate adoption of favorable policies and procedures.

In the first place, what is required is a modified theory of administrative organization. The received doctrine of administrative organization in corporations represents relatively slight modifications in the models provided by public civil and military structures. (These, too, however, do and must change.) Essentially, these structures place not only final legitimate authority for policy at the apex of a pyramid of power, but also the determination of procedures in increasing order of particularity through a chain of command. In each instance, the manager or supervisor applies policies and determines procedures for his subordinates.

The modified theory referred to would not change the final authority for policy but would change the way of determining relevant information and action. Stated in positive terms, operational decisions and the knowledge appropriate for them would be assembled where the problems arise and/or where the talent, formal training, and practical experience exist in the organization.

If this message is abstruse and therefore possibly incomprehensible, it can be made clear. In the procedures of administrative organization in accomplishing their objectives, wisdom is where you find it, and that is not necessarily correlated with position in the administrative hierarchy.

At the very least, this view argues for great flexibility in organization, consistent with the variable but generally increasing supplies of talent. The case cannot be argued here in detail, but a generalization can be put crudely and bluntly. The earlier chain-of-command theory was probably consistent, approximately, with the distribution of talent in organizations recruited from a pyramidal social order with a wide base and thin top. It is not consistent with a distribution of talent where the minimum base is very high in historical or comparative terms, and the sheer diversification of talent is extreme.

The organizational counterparts of this view of the supply of creativity are thus clear:

1. Supervisors and managers become coordinators of specialized performers, each of whom may be superior to the coordinator, each in his own field. There is no theoretical limit to this principle of organization at any rank or function.
2. Coordination then becomes itself a specialized function, capable of professionalization in terms of both skill levels and performance standards.
3. The coordinative function demands the capacity for acquiring an amateur standing in the appropriate specialties, adequate to understand their significance, balance their functions, and deflate their exaggerated claims.
4. Since a business enterprise cannot be a wholly self-governing entity, operated solely on behalf of its employed constituents, coordinators must also exercise, by delegation, reserved powers in terms of broad policies and external accountabilities for the enterprise as a whole.

Such a theory of administrative organization, if implemented, does not automatically resolve all conflicts of view and interests. Indeed, some latent conflicts may thereby become overt. It does, however, stand a chance of tapping talents not otherwise accessible.

One structural by-product of this view should be noted. Decentralization of decision making permits a substantial broadening of the coordinator's span of control (number of direct subordinates), since he is to be positively discouraged from close supervision. The geometric consequence of this change, in turn, is a flattening of the power pyramid. A functional by-product may well be a loss of tight accountabilities and some waste motion in the allocation of time to rational decision as opposed to rule of thumb or rule of the mindless intuition of superiors. But the knowledge relevant to decision, the meaningful supply of information, the exercise of rational thought are likely to be greatly enhanced.

The implementation of initiative is not simple, and since conditions for innovation may be genuinely adverse, and reasonable men may reasonably differ, some frustration is inevitable.

Policy is the balanced outcome of weighted advice and uncontrolled conditions. But the technical excellence of contributions, even though these are not practical, may still be recognized and rewarded. This is best accomplished by the technical judgment of occupational peers, for such recognition is not only a means of identification and validation of excellence but an intrinsic reward.

The employer of a professional is still a client, less knowledgeable than the practitioner and not in a position to dictate procedure. The professional attends to the judgment of his competent colleagues, and only reluctantly to his patrons. Employers and their delegated representatives would be well advised to adopt the habit of overt humility in dealings with specialists, for the latter will naturally accord them power when necessary but never competent technical authority. A professional manager may accord deference to the competence of his administrative superior, but only if he is always heard and sometimes believed.

There are all sorts of ways in which universities should be more businesslike. There are also some ways in which businesses should be more universitylike. I shall not argue these points in detail but rather offer some suggestions. Business organizations might well reconsider their emphasis on anxiety as an incentive for the maintenance of performance. On the record, anxiety is generally inconsistent with both morale and creativity, and the threat of dismissal is likely to yield only passable performance. Security of position coupled with positive rewards for excellence stand as the demonstrably superior set of conditions for linking morale and productivity. Most large business enterprises do in fact provide relative security of employment (though not necessarily of precise position) for those in the middle and upper-middle ranges of rank and income. Why not make tenure official? The inevitable mistakes may be much less costly than the loss of initiative created by fear.

The plain fact is that the history and theory of human motivation are consistently and persistently misread by the business community and most of its intellectual interpreters. *Security and initiative are positively not negatively correlated.* The current risk in business enterprise is not that office-holders have gone soft by seeking security, but that they avoid risks, including the risky business of creative thought, because they have not been accorded enough security. The freedom to disagree, to suggest improvements, to question time-honored but irrational formulas, requires for most men in most times a relatively stable place to stand. Saints and heroes are neither needed nor desirable in complex organizations. Secure and positive thinkers and doers are.

I shall state a more extreme position than I am willing to defend, for purposes of establishing a point by exaggeration. The power of corporate executives is generally exercised with restraint and even beneficence in the external world. Internally, what passes for stern justice in maintaining disciplined performance is mostly a misuse of unconscionable power that reduces the capacity of the organization and of its members to act constructively.

chapter 14

Case studies of three companies: barriers to innovation in the large organization*

Much of the discussion dealing with creativity and innovation in the business firm has tended to offer the reader a choice between believing in the omnipotence of the creative individual or considering him a passive instrument of organization forces. The choice is too narrow. In the most brontosaurian types of organizations there is mutual interaction between human participants and the institution itself. In our individualistic tradition, we naturally look for the creative individuals: the Benthams in politics, the Adam Smiths in economics, the da Vincis in imaginative and skilled expression, the Galileos in the march of human enlightenment, and the Pasteurs in the overcoming of disease.

There is certainly some validity in this emphasis. However, creativity in the industrial environment is also a function of structural design, behavioral patterns, and social pressures. The innovator in the business organization *is* constrained by organizational structure, tradition, and inertia. The individual *is* encumbered by top-heavy hierarchical structures manned by managers endowed with nebulous authority and responsibility but not possessing the power of knowledge. In fact, it may

* For the most part this chapter is the work of Ross A. Webber of the Graduate School of Business, Columbia University.

even be valid to recognize that innovation is not individual at all. With apologies to William H. Whyte, innovation may, in many respects, actually be a group activity.

Yet these criticisms of the smothering of the individual in a corporate octopus of paper forms and confusing responsibilities are too simple, too superficial. In spite of existing restrictive organization pressures, the individual is important and creative. Students of organization change have recognized the organizational pressures affecting innovation, but, as one study concluded, "at all times there was some*one* who believed in the project and pushed it." [1]

We can put the matter in another way. Some observers have challenged the assumption that initiative is a trait widely distributed throughout the population, and that the barriers which society has itself erected, especially in its large organizations, alone prevent its flowering. They indicate that a strong case may be made for the claim that most people prefer to follow; that they do not have a high degree of physical and emotional energy or the ability to take risks and deviate from established ways. The questions, though justified, only further reinforce the need to look at the influence of the organization on the individual charged with at least some responsibilities for innovation. Even our cursory research indicates that interactional energy and the ability to deviate from existing patterns are very important to innovation. But we should not ignore the roadblocks set up by the organization which put a premium on these rare attributes.

Creativity is not a "you have it or you don't" proposition. It is a continuum—a fundamental common attribute of all humanity. No organization can tap all that resides deep within the individual, and we do not want or cannot expect to make things so easy and secure that even the most timid individual will have all his views accepted. Only the incredibly naïve expect such complete and immediate responsiveness of the organization to the individual. However, whether or not a broad spectrum of humanity has innovative qualities is almost irrelevant. The important point is that the organization must not operate in a manner that poses insurmountable obstacles to all but the most creatively gifted or energetic individuals.

In the social sciences, at least, we often find it illuminating to move

[1] Harriet Ronken and Paul R. Lawrence, *Administering Changes,* Graduate School of Business Administration, Division of Research, Harvard University, Boston, Mass., 1952.

from the general to the concrete, from ideas to specific, empirical incidents and human behavior. We have been discussing the role of the individual in the large organization. What better proof of the pudding can we produce than situations which require, or at least are designed to call upon, individual initiative and creativity?

Three graduate students at Columbia's Graduate School of Business were employed in staff departments of large corporations whose objectives were somewhat similar. These departments were supposed to be agents of change for the corporations—commissioned to produce original, creative ideas that would solve existing manufacturing problems or help develop new products. In a sense, theirs is the problem which Wilbert Moore has just identified: the institutionalization of change in large organizations—getting people to develop relevant new ideas and getting the organization to accept them and put them into practice. Change is never easy; as we shall see, it is particularly difficult in large organizations.

Thus, we have here what in the physical sciences is called a "worst-case condition," requiring the personnel of a relatively small department to be influential over larger segments of the organization which typically have more prestige and a comfortable way of doing things.

Ross Webber, one of the three students mentioned and a Ph.D. candidate at Columbia, has added the studies of his two colleagues, Ralph Franke and Stephen Brown, to his own case materials.[2] However, as the reader will observe, Webber has been careful to preserve the point of view of each of the writers. We have here an opportunity to view the world of change and resistance to change from the point of view of the young engineering manager. Each is eager to show what he can do in problem solving and initiation of change; each is faced with the resistance of the organization. How does the world of work look to them? How do they rationalize their successes and failures, and more importantly, what are the common organizational factors in each of their experiences that can be identified?

Here we are in a unique position: watching highly ambitious, intelligent, technically trained young men trying to make their efforts felt in large compartmentalized organizations. What are the organizational roadblocks deterring creative responses to problems? Which are inevitable in the large organization? Which are desirable and which intolerable?

[2] These papers were prepared for my course, "Human Behavior in Organizations."

Ralph A. Franke has described a manufacturing organization in which he, as a plant technical engineer, was developing a complex gauge-and-control system to measure automatically the thickness of a chemical coating applied to plastic film.

Stephen G. Brown has recorded his experience as an assistant technologist in a major steel company research center. He observed relations between two groups which were engaged in similar applied research on coke and coal but which used different technologies.

The third case is a large chemical manufacturing organization. As a participating industrial engineer, Ross A. Webber has detailed the relationships between staff and line and their influence on innovative effort.

Although each of the studies was done independently and in very different types of companies, Webber, in the remainder of the chapter, shows us how each of the observers was struck by certain factors that were common to all three situations.

INTERGROUP COMPETITION BETWEEN STAFF GROUPS

Many companies make two contradictory assumptions, neither of which is very realistic. They assume that most experts—managers or professionals with technical backgrounds who share a common dedication to quantitative and precise methods of analysis—will be able to work together easily. After all, they are trained to be rational problem solvers. They also assume that these same people need a little competition to keep them working at top efficiency. These firms carry the concept of competition from the market place to the firm. They believe that competition between groups is conducive to getting the best out of each group.

The company had set up a management systems development division which wanted to do work which we in industrial engineering felt was our responsibility. Plant management thought that competition between groups would bring out the best efforts of both departments.[3]

---

[3] The passage quoted and others that follow are excerpts and synopses from the reports of our participant observers. No footnote references to the individual studies are given.

Our research among participants indicates that they looked upon competition as inhibitive and destructive. Continuing the above statement:

But our efforts were directed less toward doing a good job than in getting assignments and keeping them from management systems development. We spent time gathering information and performing mathematical work that the other already had completed. We jealously guarded information and seldom assisted each other.

It is interesting that there was unanimity among our participants in considering intergroup competition unproductive conflict. Franke, for example, felt that his contribution in developing a new measuring gauge would have been greater if he had access to the work of certain other groups or if he were able to control the other group in the sense that his initiation would result in predictable actions by the second group.

[Previously] I had filled a position as a development engineer in the company's engineering center and had been assigned to similar work as an officer in the Army. In both situations the work was stimulating and satisfying, and my colleagues were cordial. In both organizations the service functions like maintenance, accounting, drafting, and model shops had been *at our beck and call.* . . . Because of this experience I was unprepared for the troubles I encountered on my first job assignment after discharge from the service.

After a great deal of pressuring and bargaining, the gauge (which I was developing) was installed. However, it was not electrically wired upon installation and was still inoperative. Over two months elapsed without the wiring being connected. I would talk to production, and they would say, "See maintenance, they are the ones that have to do the work." And maintenance would say, "Talk to production. They won't shut down the equipment so that we can do the work." My supervisor would then put the pressure on: "What's holding up that project?" I would growl at the janitor when he came in the office, but what could I say or do? If I had the authority to *tell* those maintenance people to connect the wiring we could make some progress!

There is a widespread temptation among staff groups to interpret intergroup relations in conspiratorial terms: "The other staff groups are out to block what we are doing because for some reason they don't like us."

. I was a member of the plant technical group who were to work closely with production on both their short- and long-range problems. We were supposed to be the problem solvers: to find out what's wrong and decide what to do about it by running necessary tests, and then write specifications for equipment changes or additions. The specifications went to the project engineering group for the detailed design work. These specifications were a constant source of conflict between the two groups. PEG would send them back because of insufficient information and technical would claim project wanted us to do their work. Or PEG would complain technical didn't know what they were talking about, or hadn't run enough tests to justify the installation. Then technical would claim that PEG was trying to push the responsibility for possible failure off on them when it was all due to incompetent design on their part. Many volumes could be filled with examples of charges and countercharges. . . . In my view, most of the ill feeling was directed from the PEG to technical, not vice versa.

Brown has offered the suggestion that it is not competition per se which is disruptive but competition combined with fancied status differences.

I was employed as an assistant technologist in the coal-and-coke division of a steel company research center. The division was divided into two groups—Don Henredon's and Al Cohen's. Basically, both groups were supposed to test raw materials on various characteristics and write technical reports. However, their methods were based on different types of technology. . . . I became aware then of an intense rivalry existing between Don and Al's groups.

Technological differences in approach to very similar problems were the original reasons why two separate groups had been created within the division. Several years ago, all coal-and-coke testing and research was based on the method of empirical tests in the pilot coke ovens. Oven results were then used to predict the qualities of coal and coke from various sources. This method is still used by Don's group. Al Cohen became a member of this group and began to work along different technological lines. In summary, his approach endeavors to predict coke qualities from microscopic examination of coal and coke. Management split the new techniques off from Don's group and created a new group. At first the original group did not see any threat in this action. They didn't do anything either to boost their own standing or to cast aspersions on the new section. However, management began putting undue emphasis on the new technology. Cohen's group was taken out of the C building quarters it had shared with Don's group and was given an office in the A building. This was the headquarters of the research center, was air-conditioned, contained the cafeteria, and was the center of important staff activities. In comparison, the old coal-and-coke group had been placed in C building near the rear of the research center because the pilot ovens dirtied things up. The building was only infrequently visited by the director, was not air-conditioned, and housed no staff groups. From it one often had to walk to the cafeteria in the rain. Placement in A building was recognized as a symbol of considerable status.

Don's group began to be deeply critical of management's treatment of the new technology, of the superior prestige given to the group in conferences, and so forth. Often I heard Al's group referred to in unkind terms. Technologists in our group told me that the new technology wouldn't come near the correct results if we didn't run the tests our way first and submit our results along with our sample to them. There was even considerable talk about intentionally sending them erroneous reports to see if they would make errors. We were told (only half jokingly) that the main purpose of the new group was to take pretty pictures which would be shown to visitors and explained at professional conferences to impress competitors with the esoteric work that the company was doing in the field. In the opinion of our technologists, Al's group had only limited usefulness, and they were being accorded far too much recognition by research management.

I believe that the basic reason for this continuing conflict was the great status advantage accorded the new group. The technologists in Henredon's office had convinced themselves that Cohen's approach was technologically inferior to our own. If the status differential were to disappear, it is likely that as time passed, the new techniques would be accorded equal technical validity by our technicians.

Status differences between staff groups become even more destructive when the organization-caused status differentials clash with what society normally considers proper. For example, (1) older people are generally accorded more status than younger men; (2) if one group initiates work for another group that responds with a service, people think the first group has higher status; (3) if one group continuously has relations with a group of recognized high status (such as top-management personnel) while a second group does not, the first is thought to have higher status.

We see some similar problems in Franke's comments on relations between his plant technical group and a project engineering group.

The plant technical group worked closely with production and wrote specifications for equipment changes or additions. The specifications went to the project engineering group for the detailed design work. These specifications were a constant source of conflict between the two groups. . . . The PEG engineers were all older and more experienced than the technical engineers. I think they resented these younger, less experienced engineers telling them what to do, and also resented having to follow their instructions. The technical engineers also had wide contact with all levels of supervision in the plant. They were consulted by these people on problems and regularly made presentations to them. Consequently, they were well known by the people who counted, and most of the promotions to responsible supervisory positions went to them.

In summary, groups of experts find it easy to be competitive in the large organization where there is competition for status (no special pains to create it are necessary), and one cannot easily justify the assumption that competition, per se, is good for productivity. However, one caveat! We are still viewing the world from the point of view of the participant who feels frustrated that the organization does not conform more to his needs as a creative source of ideas and change. We cannot know how much of this added tension (and sense of competition) had useful by-products in spurring individuals to greater effort. Superficially at least, it seems doubtful that these goals could compensate for the losses incurred as a result of the deliberate blocking of the efforts of one individual by another who happened to be situated in a competitive group.

But another type of intergoup conflict frustrates individual initiative. We move from relations between expert or staff groups to the day-to-day work relationships between staff and line, between the individuals who are supposed to identify and solve problems by introducing changes and those who are supposed to absorb or use these in carrying on the major business functions of the organizations.

INTERGROUP COMPETITION BETWEEN STAFF AND LINE GROUPS

The very terms *staff* and *line* denote the traditional concept of the relationship between the two groups. The staff man is a box on the organization chart to one "side" of the line supervisor. He and everyone else is supposed to recognize that his efforts have no meaning aside from their use by the line manager he is serving. Yet over and over again, experience indicates that things are just not so simple. Too often the very objectives of these two types of groups seem to be in conflict.

One of our participant observers concludes wryly that what he did as a staff engineer seemed unrelated to what the production foremen were doing. The latter considered Franke's "assistance" and new equipment, which was supposed to help them, merely intrusions on their responsibilities.

During the next couple of months I spent at least sixty hours a week in the plant. The pressure on production to get the equipment installed was now turned on me to keep it in operation. A great amount of trouble persisted with the measuring part of the system. The production foreman was unwilling to take charge of the equipment and operate it as a production piece of equipment. The usual phone call would come at ten o'clock at night and I would hear, "*Your* equipment is not working. Come in and take a look at it."

A great percentage of the trouble was imagined or purposely blamed on the equipment to "explain" other troubles. Because of other pressures on the foremen, they constantly were looking for things on which to blame operating trouble.

This was a common problem for engineers. Test equipment would be blamed for every problem under the sun, and good ideas would often go down the drain for no other reason. An engineer would try to do the best possible job of explaining or "selling" the foremen and operators before the equipment was tried. This was difficult to do however, since production involved a three-shift, seven-day operation. Furthermore, most of the engineers believed that the foremen would not understand very much of the explanation since none of them were technically trained. An engineer would often come in one morning to find that the equipment he had worked three months to design and get installed had been removed because "it gave us trouble." Usually, the trouble they experienced on the run seemed totally unrelated to the new equipment.

Underlying this observer's comments seems to be a wistful inquiry, "Why should things be this way?" "Why can't production people realize that I want to help them?" However, as with conflict between staff groups, one cannot simply explain the difficulties by blaming misunderstandings caused by poor communications and the like. There are more tangible reasons for lack of cooperation.

Staff has ceased to be related to line in a purely traditional advisory relationship because of the emergence of a kind of gap between knowledge and authority. As many students of organization have pointed out, innovation, authority, and capacity to act have become increasingly fragmented in modern complex organizations. The fast pace at which knowledge accumulates has more and more concentrated technical ability and experience necessary for innovation in staff groups, not line groups.

To an increasing extent, for reasons of technical specialization that are well known, innovation is in the first instance a staff function and not in any ordinary sense an executive or entrepreneurial one. This specialization, however, heightens the universal tension between information suppliers and decision makers, that is, thinkers and doers, or in administrative language, staff and line.[4]

This fragmentation has initiated a trend toward isolation and professionalization of staff groups concerned with innovation. Staff managers become concerned with the special goals of the staff organization (e.g., increased budgets) which are not necessarily related to the needs of the groups they are advising or servicing. Webber, the observer of an industrial engineering division, comments on the role of selling staff services in the company in which he worked.

Industrial engineering, as a separate department, has formulated goals of survival for itself which are reflected in a desire to promote its own existence by obtaining additional assignments. Top staff management is constantly asking its personnel for greater effort in selling and salesmanship.

Selling places emphasis on searching for problems and getting approval to pursue them. It implies virtually a complete reversal of the behavior patterns associated with being an adviser to the line. Selling requires frequent and vigorous initiation of interaction from industrial engineering to production departments. In order to have something to sell, an engineer requires a greater order of familiarity with department problems and possibilities than he would derive from passively waiting to be consulted.

However, Webber recognizes that the individual in attempting to perform his duties cannot behave completely as staff management's emphasis on selling demands.

---

[4] See Wilbert E. Moore's contribution to this volume, Chapter 13, p. 119.

Geographic, social, and administrative factors emphasize the separation of IE as staff group from production. The emphasis on selling reinforces this by laying stress on the engineer as an outsider trying to get in. The engineer becomes aware that he must break down this identification of him as a stranger to production supervision. He must be accepted for two reasons. (1) Engaging in selling activity requires something to sell. Normally this something is an idea which has been developed after having a chance to observe production's problems. Cultivation of these ideas is a function of search, and the searching process requires an intimate knowledge of production activities. (2) It is usually not possible to maintain a significant level of projects only by selling. The engineer believes he must return somewhat to certain aspects of the traditional advisory relationship by cultivating requests for his services from the production department. The emphasis here becomes one of making himself expert and indispensable in certain areas so that the production department supervisor will naturally turn to the engineer when difficulties arise.

AMBIGUITY IN JOB REQUIREMENTS

William Foote Whyte has commented that one of the difficulties in communication between specialists and operating men is that because the intervention of the specialists tends to be sporadic, and unpredictable, its irregularity leads to a negative reaction from production supervision.[5] Geographic separations, social differences, and job duties contribute to this variable pattern. However, even more destructive of easy give-and-take relationships are the abrupt changes in the very character of the staff-line relationship.

An industrial engineer might act as an advisory staff to the department head when answering his question about whether labor cost was cheaper when baling scrap in plastic sheeting or putting loose parts in metal boxes. On another job the same engineer can act as staff to the division superintendent while checking on performance of department supervision in the matter of excess hours charged to a particular crew. On a third occasion, the engineer can exercise IE's authority over incentive plants by forcing him to accept a maximum labor hour limit on a new plan.

In oversimplified terms, in our case, the engineer does not know exactly where his job fits into the organization. Is he consultant to the chemical plant superintendent and production department head, or is he responsible

[5] William F. Whyte, *Men at Work*, Dorsey Press, Homewood, Ill., 1961, p. 561.

for the installation of measured work-control plans? In fact, he is expected to be all of these. Formal company procedure emphasizes his role as a traditional advisory staff to the superintendent. Individual engineers try to gain a position of indispensability to the department head in order to encourage initiation of requests by production supervision. They hope ultimately to improve and elaborate the relationship of engineers to production to a point where it may approach a joint consultative position in the operational structure of the production department.

The growth of professionalism in the area, the development of mathematical techniques, and the desires of new engineers all complement staff management's emphasis on innovation. This leads to a search for problems and initiation from staff to line; and these contacts are not welcomed by production personnel, who believe that staff should wait to be asked in on *their* problem. My staff department also believes that they are supposed to control incentive plans and decide what use the production department can find for them that best fits the goals of the *company* (rather than what IE might do to help production supervision best meet the production department's goals). Formal policy strengthens their hand here by assigning to IE the power to approve or disapprove all incentive standards. In addition, it is in the nature of many labor-cost control plans that they require IE to act as inspector, controller, and auditor of production-department activities. Industrial engineering sets maximum hour limits for which crews can be paid and then must approve the department heads' special wage payment request—a payment necessary for any excess hours. At least one crew exceeds the hour limits almost every week. The strains this system puts on relations between the department head and IE should be obvious. This interaction is the only one that *must* be initiated by the department head to get IE's action, and it is just the reverse of the relationship implied in a traditional advisory theory of staff.

The IE supervisor upsets the relationship in another way. To him, production units are departments to be checked and inspected to see that they are contributing to company goals according to value criteria set up by the IE division. The supervisor sits in his office checking budget figures and pay-plan performance. Whenever he has a question, he notifies an engineer to call the production department concerned and find out what happened. In this event, the engineers are forced to initiate an interaction with a department head on a matter which is obviously a justification of the manager's activities. This questioning has an adverse influence on the sentiments of the department head toward the engineer making the inquiry.

We thus see that the relationship between staff and line is characterized by confusion and inconsistency in interactional pattern and organizational roles. Both the engineer and production supervisors in the example above implicitly recognize Whyte's contention that it *is* impossible to be an inspector and a consultant at the same time.[6] The job requirements are incompatible. Therefore the staff man is left in a state of instability and flux in his relations with the people he is supposed to serve. Innovation ceases to be the prime focus of his activity. It is replaced by attempts to create for himself a position of indispensability and regularity.

CONFLICTING GROUP GOALS

It is wrong to attribute this conflict to incompatible personalities or to explain the situation in conspiratorial terms. It is also misleading to attribute to faulty communication lack of cooperation and breakdowns of information flow. Conflict is not wholly explained by ambiguity in job definition or nebulous assignment of duties. It is frequently the result of basic incongruities in the goals of the various groups and specialists who are supposed to cooperate in producing something new.

Franke's earlier example of a plant technical group engineer attempting to install a new gauge for production-quality control indicates several examples of inconsistent goals.

The reason for the urgency of my project was not related to any needs of production. They could operate quite satisfactorily without it, although costs would be slightly higher and quality somewhat lower.

The production people recalled the number of shutdowns and delays that they had experienced as a result of the efforts earlier to develop a workable production instrument. They seemed convinced that the present gauge would never work and that it was a waste of everybody's time to play around with it.

In addition, this was a difficult period for production supervision in the coating area. Since the operation was the bottleneck in the plant, the production superintendent was applying a tremendous amount of pressure there.

The installation of my equipment required a shutdown of one-sixth of the area for a two- or three-day period. Supervision was not anxious to have the coating tower down while the gauge was installed.

[6] *Ibid.*, p. 509.

In this case production supervision strongly resisted staff's attempts to install the new gauge. They felt no real need for this innovation. As new arrivals, their main concern was meeting production quotas in a bottleneck area while building up and maintaining stability in production operations and equilibrium in interpersonnel relations. The dominant pressure on them was maintenance of production at a certain rate, not cutting costs or improving quality. Certainly supervision would have liked to improve the cost picture, but for the present emphasis was on production. They considered the plant technical group and their innovation a threat to the stability they were attempting to achieve. We have already seen comments on the attitude of the foremen in refusing adequately to supervise operation of the gauge since it was "your [plant technical group's] equipment."

It was not irrational resistance to change or to the initiative of the technical specialists that prompted the production supervisors to postpone installation of the gauge system. Rather, it was a decision to deal with matters felt to be more important under existing circumstances. On the other hand, the goals of the plant technical group were not solely concentrated on realizing savings for the company. In this particular instance, Franke believes the primary motive was personal ambition.

The real push came from Phelps, the technical superintendent, who wanted to develop this system before one of the other plants. He was new to his position and of course wanted to make a good showing for the technical staff at corporate headquarters. This particular project was also of personal interest to him since it had been under his direct supervision before his promotion.

Our IE observer comments on divergent goals in similar fashion.

The goals of the foreman in solving his problems are quite different from those of the industrial engineer. The foreman is mainly interested in getting production out while maintaining stability among his personnel and equilibrium in his relations. On the other hand, the industrial engineer is busy looking for problems that are not apparent, in the hope of applying his various techniques to the modification of existing conditions. We cannot with justice say that the foremen are shortsighted while the engineers are looking ahead. The criticism is too simple, and it contains a value judgment.

We can say, with more insight, that the foremen see no real need for staff industrial engineering assistance in meeting the goals defined by the job situation and rewarded by production management.

The department head is also concerned with production, but his primary area of evaluation is on costs. Certainly his point of view is wider in scope than that of the foremen, and he is interested in innovative change. However, the heaviest pressure is still on costs, and relatively short-run costs, at that. He is not rewarded so much for long-term down trends in cost as for not exceeding weekly budgets and so on. Since industrial engineering has a major part in setting these budgets, his aims in having a loose budget clash with IE's aims in showing paper savings by cutting the budget as much as possible.

The superintendent has a greater interest in long-run costs and innovation, but he is concerned with using his own staff engineers. He maintains that their employment is cheaper, that he gets better work, and that he trains his future supervisory personnel at the same time. His desire to control all innovative proposals and to promote origination of ideas within the chemical plant division conflicts with IE's expansionist aims in the methods field.

I have pointed out the desires of both IE management and the newer engineers to broaden application of sophisticated techniques and increase the power of the staff division to initiate innovation for production supervision. We have observed that this concurrence of aims has resulted in an emphasis on *selling* industrial engineering services. Frequently the engineer, armed with his arsenal of techniques, will simply try to find a problem to which he can apply his expertise. In our case too much emphasis is being put on the techniques instead of on the problems.[7] This technical preoccupation is also a manifestation of too much concern with "professionalization"— increasing the distinctiveness and the sense of exotic intellectual activity associated with your field of specialization.

Staff management aggravates this tendency by concentrating interest on the needs of the IE division as a professional discipline. There is still much verbal declaration that industrial engineering is a service organization, but the emphasis has been subtly shifted *away* from service to the production department with its often mundane problems. Focus is on developing a discipline and serving the *company* standards as formulated by industrial engineering.

[7] The Nobel physicist, Hans Bethe of Cornell University, has commented that the use of computers has led to a tendency to think only about how to *solve* problems instead of *analyzing* the elements of the problems themselves.

Number of people and quantity of work

As with so many other considerations, the problem of oversupply of people is related to divergent goals. The growth of bureaucracy and empire building has been well presented by others and won't be repeated here. However, Brown thinks that the excess number of technologists in the research center is harmful to the quality and quantity of effort expended. In his discussion of apathy he points out the problem of differing goals and extra personnel.

The research center saw the company goals in the light of its own goals, namely, an expansion of its personnel even when it had no place to put the new people and no real jobs to give them. As long as the top management of the company continued to make funds available for expansion, research continued to expand.

This overstaffing of the center provided soil for the growth of other problems. Communications were hampered by an excessive amount of hierarchical structure. In the center alone there were five to seven levels of management, depending on whether one was a technologist or a laborer.

Our office demonstrated the physically crowded conditions at lower levels. Eight of us worked in a common area which would have been more suitable for four. A disturbance for one became a disturbance for all. The average conversational level was fairly high, and the crowded conditions put a demand on each individual's tolerance for superfluous interaction at the expense of relations needed for work. Had we been required to increase our output substantially under these conditions, we probably would have been at each others' throats constantly.

An excessive number of people results in decreased opportunity for promotion, confusion over relationships, and distorted communications; and it often encourages the less ambitious to stay on at the expense of the more ambitious who leave.

ACCESS TO INFORMATION: PHYSICAL PROBLEMS OF LOCATION

Many observers have commented on the fact that innovation requires submergence in the problem—prolonged familiarity with the elements, hard work, and extended thinking about possible alternatives.[8]

---

[8] Cf. Selections in Harold Anderson (ed.), *Creativity and Its Cultivation*, Harper & Row, Publishers, Incorporated, New York, 1959.

Thomas Edison invented more by analogy and experimentation than by imagination. He created by direct frontal assault—marshaling the widest array of facts and ideas and then carefully searching for heretofore unrecognized relationships among them. Yet today we realize that the free flow of information vital to this process is often hindered. In the steel company research center mentioned earlier, we see that intergroup rivalry between two staff groups performing very similar functions adversely affected the flow of information. It appears that each of these two research sections performing tests on the same types of raw material for the same company made every effort to *minimize* information given to the other.

In many meetings between members of the two groups, technological aspects and comparability of the two different research methods were carefully avoided as subjects of conversation. . . . When work was given to one group by the other it was never given priority except under extreme and continued pressure. . . . The joking about sending the new group results from the empirical tests has already been mentioned.

Our industrial engineering observer explicitly speaks of information flow as one of the vital necessities in staff relationships if they are to encourage innovation.

The major element in the relationship between IE and the recovery department is the extreme difficulty encountered by engineers in obtaining information. I am not repeating the old "better communications" shibboleth because it is not simply a matter of two groups misunderstanding each other. The types of information desired by IE can be divided into four categories: (1) specific production data, (2) managerial directions and letters concerning methods and procedures, (3) general running production and control data, and (4) projects reports from the development engineers. This information is wanted for two main reasons. First, the engineers cannot search for and solve problems without free access to information. This means access to data and letters that they cannot specifically ask for since they don't know beforehand what is valuable and pertinent. Second, IEs want to know what is going on in order to strengthen their position as an operating member of the production department. By making themselves indispensable they hope to increase the interaction initiated to them by the department head. The engineer in pursuing this goal will profit by having as intimate a knowledge of department activities as possible, and geographic and social isolation exercises a detrimental influence on the acquisition of this information by affecting the nature of interactions and injecting physical handicaps. All IEs are located in one office situated about three miles from most of the chemical plant operations. The trips require a wait and a bus ride taking about twenty minutes. Engineers often procrastinate about going if the weather is inclement. More important, the trip discourages all but necessary business visits. Engineers do not go out just to say hello, or to have a cup of coffee. Thus almost all interaction initiated by IEs are job-related. Indeed, engineers are generally thought of as being sticklers for work, both because of the "efficiency expert" connotation of their position and because of the job-oriented nature of their interactions.

Of course, some engineers are characterized by higher interactional energy levels than others, and these people do attempt to initiate social relations. Certain social pressures, however, hinder even these men. Age, social, and educational background differences between department heads and industrial engineers tend to be detrimental to any basis for social intercourse.

Often the engineer desires access to production records for no specific reason except that he wants to scan them or search for problem areas. Both geographic and social factors discourage the IE in this project by hindering physical access to the files, by not providing working space in the department office, and by making friendly relations with the clerk difficult to achieve. In spite of the department head's apparent willingness, the clerk has resisted giving free entrance to the files.

All these difficulties in obtaining information are not insurmountable obstacles in the path of the technical expert who wants to be a creative problem solver. In the above example, they might be overcome by frequent trips to the department, a willingness to work in inadequate surroundings in making copies of the data, and the exercise of patience. But all these activities absorb energy and diminish the engineer's attention to innovation and problem solving. It is clear that the flow of information in an innovative atmosphere consists essentially in free movement of data and memoranda, some of which is apparently superficially irrelevant, without deliberate request and without a specific purpose in mind. Valuable reflection depends on a continuous receipt of information which acts as a stimulus to the encouragement and direction of thinking. By blocking information, even a minor official can hamper the innovative process at one of its most crucial stages —the discovery of a problem.

IMPACT OF SUPERVISORY PATTERNS AND ADMINISTRATIVE METHODS

The previous sections have dealt with organizational or *structural* defects which impede individual contributions to the success of the firm. Most are a product of the division of labor, the formation of separate departments which evolve distinct and often incompatible subgoals for themselves and frequently fail to intermesh or complement one another's activities. There are other problems caused by inept administration.

Influence of supervisory style

Because of our historic emphasis on the individual and the importance of personal leadership, studies of supervisory styles have been popular for a number of years. Early questioning of autocratic methods led many "enlightened" students and administrators to jump to the conclusion that "free" or "general" supervision was more conducive to productivity and morale. More recent studies have led to serious questioning of this equating of morale and leadership style with productivity of workers.[9] However, this question of general supervision and productivity has not been seriously extended to areas where the functions of the supervised require creativity. Assuming that innovation requires a free, uninhibited flow of activity and interaction because it relies on borrowing and analogy, observers have argued that a free intellectual atmosphere similar to that in a university is most conducive to innovative thinking.[10] Our participant observers do not completely agree with these views.

As a plant technical engineer, Franke apparently liked freedom from supervision for his technical work on the coating gauge, but he decries a lack of supervision for nontechnical activities.

[9] Cf. Studies of the Survey Research Center, University of Michigan, Ann Arbor, Mich.: Katz, Maccaby, and Morse, *Productivity, Supervision, and Morale in an Office Situation*, 1950; Katz, Maccoby, Gurin, and Floor, *Productivity, Supervision, and Morale among Railroad Workers*, 1951; Donald Pelz, *Power and Leadership in the First-line Supervisor*, 1951.

[10] Cf. Henry Eyring, "Scientific Creativity," in Anderson, *op. cit.*, pp. 2–12, and Simon Marcson, *The Scientist in American Industry*, Industrial Relations Section, Princeton University, Princeton, N.J., 1960.

I rarely saw my supervisor except when he spent a little time to give me another assignment, or rare checks on the progress of a past assignment. Since the big technical push was in another area, I was practically unsupervised. I felt this was a considerable disadvantage because an engineering supervisor can acquaint a new man with a lot of the details about the work situation and can help him on the nontechnical problems that the engineer hasn't been successful in handling.

Absence of supervision is a disadvantage here because the subordinate feels weak without someone to strengthen him in his dealings with production supervision and other departments. Franke wants someone with leverage to whom he can go for assistance.

In the contemporary organization, supervision, little or great, does not only emanate from one's supervisor. One feels pressures (or their absence) from individuals and groups who precede or follow one's position in the flow of work. Orthodox theory again would suggest that individuals don't want pressure; they want to be left alone. But again this easy-to-accept principle in human relations is not borne out so simply by our observers. As Webber notes:

Both I and my colleagues welcomed some work pressures from other groups around us, particularly from the production departments we were supposed to be serving. The pressures from line management give the engineers a sense of "belonging" to the production department and of their work being important enough to warrant interest. In this particular situation, line pressure usually does indicate that the IE's assignment is important. The engineers respond with extra hours of work and additional effort. Of course, the extra effort demonstrated is also related to the fact that the engineer has been in the spotlight and knows it. His conspicuousness presents an opportunity to build a reputation on something considered valuable.

Brown, in his coal-and-coke research department, was also critical of the excessive passivity of his supervisor. He observed that since the manager did nothing to relieve the rivalry between the two major subgroups in his department, his men thought him weak and ineffectual. In turn their contempt contributed to still further animosity within the department.

On the other hand, in the industrial engineering department, Webber experienced the disadvantages of excessively close supervision. The effects he felt at the time are graphically and emotionally described in this excerpt from his report:

There is widespread discontent among staff engineers because of the detailed supervision they receive on their technical work from the manager. He has been incapable of refraining from criticizing aspects of a new idea even before the whole plan is presented or thought out. This action tends to hinder progress on all innovative ideas and to destroy others completely. Of course, one can complain that the engineers should be stronger individuals in standing up for their ideas; but excessively critical evaluation of an idea at an early stage can convince the originator it is not likely to be a fruitful course of action. This is not caused by a weakness in the engineer's personality, but is due to the natural frailty of all new conceptions. The creator has simply not been able to envision all the facets of his idea and is incapable of defending it in the earliest stages.

The adverse effects of close supervision are not reflected in low productivity (or at least in pace or diligence) so much as in a redirection of effort to items of less importance. Franke, for example, supplied an example of wasteful redirection of effort. Unreasonable criticism of one of his drawings caused him to devote extraordinary time to redrawing it to excessive perfection—a step which did not contribute to progress on the job. In the industrial engineering division, close supervision is also reflected in emphasis on "selling," getting new jobs for yourself, and applying the esoteric mathematical techniques we have already discussed.

The key to the possible coexistence of close supervision and zest for work in the IE division, however, was found in its past record of rapid promotions. The division historically had served as a training ground for the whole company.

There may be some correlation between closeness of supervision and opportunity for promotion. This industrial engineering division always had too many supervisors with little to do except supervise subordinate engineers. Although the engineers haven't welcomed this supervision (and indeed, most of the supervisors haven't enjoyed it), it has tended to provide rapid promotional opportunities and "paper" supervisory experience for the engineer's record. Close supervision coupled with frequent evaluation for possible promotion has prevented apathy.

Monitoring work

Evaluating creative personnel for promotion brings us to the question
of how the supervisor monitors or measures the performance of subordinates. Webber implies that his colleagues traded greater freedom
in their work for closer supervision (and he implies, a greater quantity
of information on who is promotable). On the other hand, Brown
observed that managers in the steel company's research department
were reluctant to exercise this type of supervision, although they also
believed they lost something as a result: adequate information about
what was going on. Parenthetically, it is interesting to note that the
subordinates in the research center were apathetic, while Webber
reports that he and his fellow engineers were enthusiastic and had
"high morale."

Clearly the measurement process affects the quantity of initiative
and originality the subordinate will demonstrate in performance. What
is he rewarded for? What is he punished for? How consistent and
reliable is the reward-and-punishment system?

The steel company research center's managers relied on the number
of completed research reports as a measure of "how things were
going." In fact, each research group had a quota. Yet the men recognized that a quota of reports was a poor control in a research environment, and that numbers alone could never reflect the "numerous
technical and human variables which affect a research project."

Because they did not accept the validity of this control and believed
that their managers knew little else about their work, "there was widespread apathy and resignation."

The research center's production was measured in completed research
reports, and a quota existed for each research group. That the quota system
was not proving very effective was evidenced by the fact that it was only
loosely adhered to. It was a poor statistical control because it failed to
consider the numerous technical and human variables which affect a research
project. The supervisors on all levels also used personal contacts in supervision but appeared to be torn between their need for knowledge of group
working norms and their dislike for constantly looking over the shoulders
of their subordinates.

I had been working in the coal-and-coke division only a few days when
I began to realize that seldom was anyone in a hurry to accomplish anything. . . . Laborers and technologists alike loafed and made few attempts

to cover up. . . . One man liked to say that he told each new, hardworking technologist that he had six months. This meant that even the most conscientious new man would soon become aware of the needlessness and futility of working hard.

The men who could ignore the working conditions, who could shut out the noisy argument or discussion going on around them and tend to their work in a routine fashion were the ones who lasted the longest and eventually were promoted. . . . They were fairly quiet individuals and rarely tried to exercise any leadership in the group. They were neither too ambitious nor too questioning. The ones who thought they could do very good work lost their interest fairly quickly.

The eventual promotion by seniority of those without demonstrated desire to be active and initiate interactions led to less than optimal supervision at lower levels.

Thus the reward system favored the plodder.

"Management by results" is a meaningless phrase for most staff work.[11] In the first place, on projects of a research nature, even the most optimistic cannot expect a very high percentage of "successful" results. Emphasis ought rather to be on evaluating and controlling progress within certain limits, so that managers may determine whether the organization system is operating properly and moving toward a successful outcome or whether a new direction should be pursued *before* a bad result occurs. Similarly, on more orthodox staff-service functions, results are often far removed from the staff's activity and are virtually useless as a control technique. In the steel company research center we saw that there were fears about relative status and management recognition between two groups working along similar lines. The situation was characterized by an almost complete lack of adequate monitoring. The real control appears to be a requirement for a certain number of technical reports each year.

In order to set some sort of standard, the director of the research center had made it known that each group was expected to publish each year approximately three times as many blue books (reports) as it had technologists. Our technologist confided to Ed and me that each of them had

---

[11] Management by results means an absence of continuous monitoring in favor of checking "results" at the time of actual completion. The argument is that if the goals are met, the superior need not be concerned with the methods used by subordinate supervisors, thus ensuring freedom and flexibility of operation for the subordinates.

one or two things in his desk that he could make into a blue book within a week if he had to.

Some of the "irrational" behavior in intergroup relations is related to the inability to monitor staff operations: for example, the efforts to look important, to get to some position, or to present an idea ahead of another group in order to keep them from "looking good."

The difficulty in monitoring performance also contributes to the confusion, which was mentioned earlier, in the relationships between staff and line in the industrial engineering department.

Industrial engineering management had historically used "savings" supposedly produced by IE projects for evaluation purposes. Over the years, however, it became apparent that these cost savings were less an indication of the individual engineer's work than merely a summation of all the changes which the production department had installed since the last IE study. Nonetheless, paper savings still are a factor in evaluating IE performance, and the individual pays substantial attention to them.

Production department evaluation of industrial engineering activities was even more nebulous. Realizing the uselessness of claimed cost savings, production supervision evaluated IE for its service contribution—estimating how much they eased the job of the manager.

Our discussion of conflicting goals indicates that IE management's evaluation on the basis of savings from innovation may directly clash with production management's evaluation of the engineer's help to them in meeting operational problems, including day-to-day maintenance of work regularity. The engineer finds that he is not sure which management he is to satisfy and under what standards of evaluation.

On the one hand, IE supervision controls his pay raises and promotion in industrial engineering. On the other, the engineers have normally been young people with line-management aspirations. Transfers out of the division have depended on being requested by the production departments. The lack of objective criteria for monitoring the engineer's innovative work leads him to transfer his main attention from the quality of his ideas to attempts to find out whom to please and how.

Here we see how monitoring or controls can also affect intergroup relations, not only superior-subordinate relations. How well a group that is supposed to facilitate the work of another group actually performs this function depends upon how each is being measured and rewarded.

Webber comments that his department had a structural problem, which we have already referred to: excessive numbers of personnel. Under one system of monitoring, where individual production departments were not charged for the time of engineers who worked for them, one effect was produced. But when top management changed its measures so as to charge production units for the engineer's services, quite a change in attitude and behavior occurred.

Since the division had historically been used as a training area for new technical managerial personnel, the excessive number of people was not a handicap. Effort was all too often concentrated on trivia, but the work did offer experience (and facilitated individual promotions), and since the individual production departments were not charged for IE time, they did not complain.

Plant management changed the budgeting of industrial engineering from a charge against general plant overhead to a system which charged IE hours on each assignment directly to the production department concerned. Because of this step, production supervision began to question closely the quality and contribution of IE services. Staff management began to feel that the young engineers could not develop enough ability to perform optimal engineering work in the short time they had been staying in the department. The decision was made to emphasize career opportunities in industrial engineering and to cut down on promotions out of the department in order to build up the experience level. This change had a harmful effect on employee morale. The division was filled with bright, frustrated people because of the seriously curtailed promotional opportunities.

CONCLUSION

This chapter has endeavored to summarize three case studies of departments that were supposed to be creative and to tap the initiative and ingenuity of their employees. As we have seen, their relative success and failure was a function of some rather sophisticated interrelationships between groups and between supervisors and subordinates. Simple homilies about leaving the creative person on his own, supervising by results, making one department the source of creative ideas and leaving the other to do the routine production work—just aren't successful. They neglect the realities of organization life, the challenges posed by a division of labor which requires individuals and groups to intermesh their activities.

Individual creativity and initiative are as much functions of structural and administrative technique as of individual competence. Surely the brain power and skill of the individual is necessary, but it can be useful only in so far as management can comprehend the subtleties of organizational behavior.

The picture of the large corporation that Webber and his associates have given us is far different from one imagined by the armchair theorists. As Harlan Cleveland has told us in Chapter 2, the organization is no hegemony. We don't find people being swaddled by excessive security or manipulative supervisors. Excessive bureaucratization is much less of a problem than its opposite: an absence of regularity, of clarity of job assignment, or of harmonious interlocking of managerial positions. Rather than a stifling atmosphere of peace and quiet, the modern organization has a good deal of internal conflict. The individual has ample opportunity to express his individuality, but the usefulness of that expression depends upon the degree to which excessive intergroup competitiveness and conflict can be moderated. However, the creative employee who expects that the wisdom of his ideas will carry them to acceptance is being deluded. As distinct from the solitary scholar putting pen to paper and waiting for the world to read and marvel, the member of the organization must depend upon his skills for comprehending the patterning of human relationships and being able to cope with them.

chapter 15

Defining work in
organizational terms*

The cases cited in the preceding chapter illustrate the problems created by ambiguous relationships. In spite of this obvious ambiguity it is often assumed—and we would say naïvely—that an inverse relationship exists between the amount of structure of explicit rule making in an organization and the amount of freedom or room for initiative enjoyed by individual members of that institution. This view assumes that these conditions—control and freedom—are, in fact, opposite ends of a continuum. Obviously this is not true. Unfortunately the view is widely held, and it influences a great many decisions of those inside the organization as well as those outside who are predicting its impact on people.

An English businessman, Wilfred Brown, who heads a bearing-manufacturing company, has recently explored the relationship between individual initiative and organization controls. He finds that the modern organization, because of the extreme interdependence among its manifold activities, requires limitations on the discretion of the individual. Brown has observed that most business organiza-

* Except for the introduction, the material in this chapter is taken from Wilfred Brown, "What is Work?" *Harvard Business Review,* vol. 40, no. 5, pp. 121–128, September–October, 1962. Some sections of the article have been deleted.

tions err on the side of failing to be explicit about the work required of their employees. They speak in glib terms about "responsibility" for this or that, as though the individual was working by himself, when, in fact, work involves fitting into an organizational framework. But paradoxically, Brown shows us that a recognition of the real organizational limits on individual initiative does not throttle the employee. Realistic definitions of jobs serve to stimulate effective employee contributions. Here we have also a good opportunity to examine systematically the nature of work—the meaning of a job— in the context of the organization.

WHAT IS WORK?

Businessmen, in general, simply do not understand the exact meaning of the term *work*. People in industry have not yet reached the stage where they talk about work in objective terms. . . . Many of our attempts to describe *work* are nothing more than descriptions of the *people* who do the work. . . . For example, we refer in airy terms to managerial work, accounting work, skilled or unskilled work, and engineering work, and sometimes to boring work or interesting work, and so on. Obviously these are terms which are more descriptive of the type of person who does the work or his state of mind while working than of anything else.

Nor are we any better off if we move just one step closer to a specific definition. Suppose we say, as many companies do, that Mr. X is responsible for production or for sales. Are we not still misstating the facts? It is the board of directors who actually is responsible for seeing that these functions are adequately performed . . . at the many levels of the corporation. Separate individuals, subordinate to the president, work exclusively in the area of production or sales.

But as one descends the hierarchy of organization, it is clear that every person in the enterprise is responsible for some sort of work that is connected with these basic functions. Therefore, to say that Mr. X is responsible for sales or Mr. Y for production tells one nothing about the work either does. The real question is: What distinctive part of production work does Mr. Y do and in what terms is it to be described so as to distinguish it from the work done on production by other people in the company?

Better breakdown

One answer has been suggested by the findings of the Glacier Project, so called because it was conducted in my company, the Glacier Metal Company, Limited, which indicate that the work of any role can be objectively and distinguishably described in terms of its *prescribed* and *discretionary* content.[1]

By *prescribed* content we mean the things that the occupant of the role must do if he is to avoid a charge of negligence or insubordination. One of the characteristics of prescribed work is that one knows when he has completed it. For example, a manager may prescribe that his subordinate produce for him each month a written report in four parts, detailing:

- Results of operations for the month
- Developments in hand
- Recommendations for changes
- Problems on which assistance is required

Although the content of the report is largely at the dictate of the subordinate's judgment (i.e., discretionary), there is no discretion given as to whether or not he renders such a report, and he certainly will know whether or not he has complied with the instruction. The manager may, after receiving the report, criticize its content as a display of substandard use of discretion, but he cannot accuse its writer of insubordination if it is on his desk at the due date.

On the other hand, *discretionary* work is composed of all those decisions that we not only are authorized to make but also are held responsible for making. As soon as a man grows familiar with this

[1] In 1948 Glacier Metal Company, Limited, in collaboration with the Tavistock Institute of Human Relations, London, initiated a joint sociological project for the study of organization, supported by government research funds. This continued for three years, and at the end of that period, Dr. Elliott Jaques, who led the original project, assumed the position of independent sociological consultant to the company; and the research continued, having a life so far of fourteen years. For other findings stemming from this study, see the article by Dr. Jaques, "Objective Measures for Pay Differentials," Harvard Business Review, January–February 1962, p. 139. Also see *Exploration in Management,* by Wilfred Brown, 1960, and *Equitable Payment,* by Elliott Jaques, 1961—both books published by John Wiley & Sons, Inc., New York, and by Heinemann Educational Books, Ltd., London.

way of thinking about work, it becomes clear that although the mere carrying out of the prescribed content of work is the *sine qua non* of retaining the job, he earns no medals simply for obeying instructions. If he doesn't, he gets fired! Ideally in business, we are judged to be good, indifferent, or poor, on the basis of the quality of our decision making.

Discretion in decisions

Many people in industry feel that the "top brass" make all the decisions and that factory and office workers only do *routine* work which does not involve the use of discretion. Any objective analysis of a specific job, however, soon explodes this assumption. Take, for example, a filing clerk's job. Surely, we might think that there are no decisions to be made in this situation. But this is not so. For example, a filing clerk might spend considerable time in deciding:

- How to rate concurrent demands for filing service coming from several sources at the same time, that is, how to decide which should be met first
- Whether to go to his supervisor and ask for assistance to meet a temporary flood of work, or to allow himself to get temporarily into arrears
- When to open new files for correspondence which was previously filed under a bulging "miscellaneous" category
- Whether particular documents are or are not intended for filing in his center
- How to develop original work methods in order to get through more quickly

Immediate availability of back correspondence is very important to managers, but even the most thoroughly prescribed routine will not ensure this, because much depends on the wise use of discretion by filing clerks.[2]

[2] Interestingly, a recent study of new managers identifies one of the most successful as a young engineer who was assigned the job of maintaining a file of reports for a vice-president. His initiative in converting this routine, uninteresting "dogwork" type of job into a challenge—by developing original indexes and techniques for updating the file—made a superb impression on his boss. It was an important step in his rapid promotion in the company. Cf. W. R. Dill, T. L. Hilton, and W. R. Reitman, *The New Managers,* Prentice-Hall, Inc., Englewood Cliffs, N.J., 1962, pp. 39 ff. (This footnote, not in Mr. Brown's original article, was added by Sayles.)

Differences in responsibility

There are decisions being made at all levels in a company. Further proof of this is shown by the fact that a manager will allocate work of varying difficulty to subordinates (all of whom, superficially, are doing the same type of work) on the basis of his personal confidence in their individual capacities to make what he assesses as wise decisions. Actually, then, since each employee is given different levels of assignment, everyone does not have the *same* job, despite the fact that an individual may be labeled a tool designer, or an assistant director of marketing, or what have you. Therefore, if the employee who bears the most responsibility is not paid more than ones with less responsibility, a sense of injustice may properly arise. The best man should be rewarded fairly, while the manager should assist the other subordinates in developing their own competence. . . .

Gains through explicitness

I am trying to behave like a scientist; for the main task of science is to describe the world in which we live in ever more precise generalities. There is, however, some advocacy in my remarks, for I believe it to be important that, as far as possible, we cease relying on intuitive knowledge and attempt to make this knowledge explicit in our minds, at least. Thus, it would seem to me to be a substantial contribution toward the effectiveness of the way in which we operate industry, if:

- Every manager could be more formally aware of the prescribed bounds within which he is working and the decisions which he alone is responsible for making
- Managers became explicitly aware of the policies they set which bound the area of discretion allocated to *their* subordinates

In our company, we have found it helpful, when a job falls vacant, to draft a specification of the *prescribed* and *discretionary* content of the optimum level of work which the manager in charge of that role will want the appointee to be able to perform. Those who become alarmed at this procedure often assume that the specifications remain static and are unchangeable by the manager. They assume, further, that such specification necessarily would *curtail* opportunity for a display of initiative and insight by the person in the role, which would introduce a degree of rigidity into the organization and inhibit the growth in the amount of responsibility taken on by its members.

One of these questioners went so far as to say:

The manager in charge of that part of our organization responsible for development of new products feels free to use his and his staff's inventive genius to think up new products and to spend resources in developing them that would keep our company ahead of competition, without going to his boss every time to ask if he can go ahead. If his role were tightly prescribed, he could not do this.

My reply to him was this:

A wise chief executive prescribes the role of the manager responsible for the development of new products by stating that he has a budget within which he must work. If he feels that the interests of the company are best served by spending beyond this, he has the *duty* of raising the matter with the chief executive. He has an establishment of personnel, plant, factory, office space, and so on which are available to him. And he works within a wide range of coordinating policies which are set by the chief executive. Within such prescribed limits, he is charged with the responsibility of making decisions to optimize the probability of our products keeping ahead of competition. He also knows that if the company does fall behind, he is liable to be assessed as having shown poor judgment and, in the last analysis, will lose his job.

Under these circumstances I think that there is less danger of the product-development man in our company falling down on his job than there is that his counterpart in the company of my questioner will be unsuccessful.

BOUNDARIES ON DECISIONS

In a large company employing thousands of people, work has to be integrated toward the development, production, and sale of a broad range of products or services. Unless prescribed boundaries are set on the decisions that each individual can make, it is impossible to get each one of those thousands working toward a common end. For example, if the company is developing an airplane, then the president must lay down the general specifications for construction:

■ Is it to be a small executive aircraft or a 150-passenger airliner?
■ What is its flight range to be?
■ What is to be its weight, general performance, and the like?

If the president does not do this, his immediate subordinate who is responsible only for design may well go astray and produce something that does not fit the company's manufacturing capacity or is unsuitable for sale in the particular sector of the market in which the company is operating. Within the general specifications as to the type of plane, performance requirements, ultimate market, and so forth laid down by the president, the manager who is responsible for design must split up the job between his subordinates. He has to set prescribed limits on each of the subassemblies which he delegates to each of a number of subordinates so that those subassemblies will fit together in the total aircraft. If one man is responsible for the landing gear, he must see its relationship to the main fuselage; while the man in charge of tail design must envisage its relationship to the wing areas. Thus, all parts of the main task must be prescribed in such a way as to make them fit together.

Now, this can be clearly seen with regard to the task of designing a complex product. But the same prescribed boundaries on decisions are not so easily approved when applied to the framework of policies regarding the use of resources, pay, hours of work, status, and services within which every person in an organization must work. It should, however, be clear to those who have management experience that unless top management sets coordinating policies which prescribe the discretion of managers throughout the company, individual managers would be entitled to make decisions that could create chaos.

For instance:

■ If one departmental manager is allowed to approve excessive overtime while another has to lay off a number of people, serious trouble will arise.
■ If a superintendent decides to reward a particular type of work at a level of pay which differs substantially from that paid for similar work in other departments, then pressures are set up for every other department to follow suit.
■ If one office manager provides all staff working at a particular level with private offices and other office managers do not, then considerable emotional pressures arise in the company.

Clearly, therefore, some generalized control with regard to many aspects of business has to be brought into existence to prevent these things from happening.

FREEDOM WITHIN THE LAW

There is a widely accepted (though seldom stated) policy in industry about organization, which runs something like this:

Do not formalize the work of specific jobs closely, for in appointing people to these roles, one has no means of prediscovering the differential ability of people, and therefore it is best to leave each individual to assume the maximum responsibility which he himself feels capable of discharging. By creating this situation, the innate intelligence and personality of each employed person will determine the work which he does, and this will ensure that the fullest use will be made of the capacity of the people employed.

Although I recognize the controversial nature of my belief, I strongly feel that this doctrine is quite unrealistic. I contend that the work of all jobs *is* bounded by prescribed policies. The only question is one of an explicit recognition of the bounds.

Many management theorists and sociologists use the categories *formal* and *informal* when talking about organization. Most of them approve of informal organization because "it provides freedom of action for the individual." But I suggest that there is a fundamental error in their thinking, based on their failure to perceive that all human work involves the use of judgment, choice, or discretion. As soon as human judgment is *not* required to get work done, then that work is mechanized. You can think up hypothetical jobs which involve no discretion, but you will not find them in reality. If this fact is not recognized, then it is easy to assume that a completely formalized or explicit organization deprives everybody of freedom to act.[3]

Anxiety without bounds

If nothing is formalized in an organization (if there are no written or explicitly recognized prescribed bounds to the work roles), then

[3] Cf. Ivar Berg's discussion, in Chapter 5, of the leeway provided for employee maneuvers to build in initiative for increased job satisfaction. Of course, as Berg notes, the initiative need not contribute to greater organizational effectiveness.

clearly no one really knows what decisions he or anybody else is authorized to make. Every time an individual in the company faces a problem, his first thought would have to be, "Is it my responsibility to deal with this or is it not?" In the absence of prescribed bounds to his role, he does not and cannot know. Therefore, he will have to decide first whether or not to act. Then, if he decides to do so, he will have to make a decision on what action to take. But once he has made his decision, others may question his right to do so. His manager may "bawl him out" or may praise him for "showing initiative"; the individual does not know in advance which response he will get.

Making decisions is always difficult because there is always a lapse of time before we know whether or not we have acted wisely. But if we are to be judged, on every occasion, not only on the wisdom of our decisions themselves, but also on whether or not we were correct in assuming that the responsibility was or was not within our authority, then our work lives will be intolerable. We will lie in a state of constant uncertainty about our own duties, which would unfortunately affect our work.

I personally believe that the more formalization that exists, the more clearly we will know the bounds of the discretion which we are authorized to use *and will be held responsible* for using. Formalization of organization delineates authority or roles, and prescribed policies make clear to people the area in which they have freedom to act. Without a clearly defined area of freedom, there is no freedom. This, in fact, is a very old story reaching down through the history of mankind: *There is no real freedom without laws.*

Some readers may tend to reject these ideas because the corporation that is their employer has no explicit policies—a circumstance enabling them to assume (through sheer courage) an ever greater responsibility. But these readers may remember that if one of their colleagues wants to usurp some of their responsibility through equal courage and initiative, then, according to their own set of rules, that colleague is entitled to do so! Presumably, an interesting battle will result! Likewise, if some of their subordinates decide to stop doing the job the superior expects of them, then what, according to their set of rules, should they do? It seems to me that they must either let the situation ride (which would be disastrous from a work point of view), or else move in and prescribe the work content of their subordinates' roles.

In short, there are always prescribed bounds to roles in organizations, but often they are not explicit. When they are not, there is an endless possibility of political maneuvers by company employees.

MANAGING CHANGE

Nowadays in business there is much talk about resistance to change. But change always involves alteration of existing policy. If a policy is not explicit in the first place, then changes are difficult, if not impossible, to articulate. Suppose that a plant manager faces a steady and dangerous rise in the level of expense in consumable supplies. He wants to halt this advance and eventually bring the expense back to a level which he considers to be reasonable. However, he has formulated no policy on the subject before, so that he does not know how many employees at various levels throughout the company are responsible for all the thousands of decisions which cause the expense. Thus, the first thing he must *do is to determine which* roles are authorized to *use discretion* to expend these supplies. In other words, *the prelude to effective change is to make existing policy explicit.*

The plant manager who does not cause this to be done may, instead, make assumptions about who is responsible for such expenditure; but if his assumptions are inaccurate, then his change of policy will be ineffective as well. Unless there is a reasonably accurate and well-defined appreciation of the current situation in the mind of the manager who wishes to introduce change, the decisions he makes about what is to be changed are likely to be inconsistent with reality. Consequently, his subordinates will act puzzled and anxious, and they will probably begin to resist change. If the manager adopts the conventional outlook, he will probably think his subordinates are obstinate, anxious, lacking enough imagination to see the benefits arising out of his ideas. This would be quite unfair.

I am not suggesting that there is no such thing as genuine resistance to change, but it is clear to me that much of the seemingly uncooperative behavior of people is due to their genuine concern about the operational folly of the proposed changes stemming from the lack of insight into the reality of the situation. Thus some resistance to change is a result of organization and not of the character of people. . . .

CONCLUSION

The study of management is not merely a study of man, involving an understanding of his character, his motivation, his aims, and his behavior in different circumstances. Such a study involves the structure of roles which make up an organization, the work content of those roles, the relationship among roles, and the manner in which this structure of roles and their work content should be adapted to the environment in which a company operates.

It is not sufficient that managers recognize only the psychological aspects of work. They must understand (and be able to describe) how work is bounded by organizational policies. By pretending that such limitations to our work do not exist—on the basis that by so doing we give initiative free rein—we often end up with employees who, undecided about whose job it is to catch the ball, allow it to fall between them.

By contrast, managers who define jobs objectively in terms of their *prescribed* and *discretionary* content and who are aware of how the policies they themselves set impinge on and bound the area of discretion of their subordinates, will find that they have far fewer organizational and human relations problems to contend with.

Managerial training

This more realistic view of the nature of work has a further and vitally important implication for the many institutions whose efforts are devoted to the training of managers. I am convinced that such training tends to emphasize the supposed irreconcilability of the organizational and the psychological aspects of management, and I am equally strongly convinced that a thorough study of management would in fact show that these two views are not irreconcilable after all.

When, in this article, I have argued that the behavior of an individual at work is partially a function of his structural position in the organization and the work content of his role, this does not mean that I deny the influence of psychological factors. As a matter of fact, I am quite willing to admit that:

■ Different people put into the same role will behave in different fashions.
■ Increasing the efficiency and bettering the relationships among people

in various roles are also functions of the character and personality of the individuals concerned.

■ The actual work established in any particular role must be varied (within authorized brackets) according to the capacity for work of the individual in that role.

What I would like to see, on the part of those involved in management training, is an equal willingness to admit the influence of organizational factors.

The training of managers should be concerned with *both* the psychological aspects of management *and* the sociological aspects of organization. To treat these as mutually exclusive alternatives is to try to construct a bicycle with one wheel. That many institutions concerned with the training of managers ignore the organizational aspects of the subject to an alarming extent is evidenced by the fact that they are without definitions of such social entities as manager, specialist, work, representative, policy, instruction, and so on—without, in effect, the kind of vocabulary of clearly bounded terms which has proved so essential to the teaching of the physical sciences. Without such a necessary means of communication about organization, how can a body of knowledge emerge? And in the absence of knowledge, how can teaching proceed very far?

chapter 16

Structural and administrative innovations that motivate people*

Moving away from the qualities of the individuals attracted to and retained by the organization, we are interested in the use of the organization itself as a structure to further the growth and development of the individual and his contribution to the goals of the business. As we have already noted, Professor Whyte is probably one of the best-known social scientists grappling with the relationship of organizational variables and individual performance. Let us turn to his assessment of the state of our current knowledge about structure and administration as they affect human behavior.

No single pattern of adjustment between man and organization can be discerned even among large companies in our society. While no organization provides a setting in which members do just as they please, we find that some organizations press members into conformity whereas others apparently liberate the creative energies of the members. It seems pointless to me to argue whether the "average" business organization stifles or promotes creativity. On the other hand, if we analyze the conditions which seem to stifle or promote creativity, we

* Except for the introduction, this chapter is by Prof. William F. Whyte and follows the materials he presented at the conference.

may learn how to make possible individual expression in our organizations.

THE IMPACT OF TASK
AND TECHNOLOGY

At the outset, we must recognize that it is not men alone who constitute the oppressive or liberating atmosphere of the organization. The task the organization is set up to accomplish and the technology and work flow through which this task is accomplished may have important impacts upon individual freedom of action.

The automotive assembly line presents an extreme example of the control of behavior by technology and work flow. As Charles Walker and his associates have pointed out, the worker on the line is limited to a few simple physical motions which he repeats over and over all day long. Except for brief relief periods, his physical position is determined within a few square feet of space by the line and his function on it. Furthermore, his social interaction while at work is drastically limited to those in immediately adjoining positions on the line.

We can hardly be surprised to find such assembly-line workers lamenting their lack of freedom of action and their enforced conformity to management standards. However, it is noteworthy that they do not attribute their unhappy job situation to their immediate supervisor. He may be a good guy or not—his personality will make some difference to them—but they recognize that the technology rather than the foreman is enforcing their conforming behavior.

The structure of the organization is now also thought to have an important impact upon individual freedom of action. Decentralization of authority means, in effect, allowing people to make their own decisions in their own spheres of activity. In management thinking, this decentralization is associated with the notion of supervision by results: The individual is not checked step by step on the procedures he follows; instead, he is given a wide range of choice among procedures and is rewarded or punished according to the results he achieves.

While these are sound notions in general, we must recognize that a philosophy of decentralization or supervision by results is more easily implemented in some types of organization than in others. For example, the retail stores of Sears Roebuck and Company are widely known in management literature for decentralization of authority (few organizational levels from top to bottom and a wide span of control, making detailed supervision difficult). Supervision by results also seems to be a prominent feature of Sears's management approach in this part of their operation.

Without trying to minimize the Sears Roebuck achievement, we should recognize that the task and technology have enabled the company to go much further in these directions than may be possible for other firms with different tasks and technologies. The departments and divisions of the stores are almost totally independent of each other, so that management does not have to face the complex problems of work flow and interdepartmental coordination found in some other types of business. Furthermore, selling results are relatively easy to measure and are, in fact, measured in standardized fashion. The supervisor receives on his desk at regular intervals a set of figures that represent reasonably well the results for each selling division. Scanning these figures, he looks for any marked deviations, comparing one division with another and the present with the past record in each division. Where deviations occur, the boss initiates discussions with the responsible subordinate. Where the figures show good and consistent results, the boss can afford to let well enough alone.

A man may take a rather unorthodox approach to running his division, but if he shows good results, it is difficult for his boss to tell him that he is not behaving as an organization man should. Perhaps the admitted success of certain unconventional methods helps to explain why the buyer in some large department stores is even expected to be temperamental and something of a screwball.

Compare this situation with what we observe, for example, in the oil industry. In a large producing field we have a bewildering array of highly interrelated activities: drilling, producing, pipelines, maintenance and construction, power supply, engineering, geology, and others. For every man directly involved in drilling, producing, or shipping, there may be as many as two men in auxiliary services. Vital though it is, their contribution cannot be directly measured. Even the task of measuring the performance of those directly involved with the oil presents exceedingly difficult problems. The figures on labor, material, and other costs are of course available, but since no one oil field is just like any other oil field, an important amount of managerial judgment always enters into evaluating how good or bad the cost and production records are. This analysis suggests several management postulates:

1. The more difficult it is to evaluate results, the more difficult it is to supervise on the basis of results.
2. The more difficult it is to evaluate results, the more likely we are to find a pattern of close supervision and a relatively small number of subordinates reporting to a given superior.
3. The difficulty of evaluating results will vary with (*a*) the nature of the mission of the organization and (*b*) the adequacy of the reporting systems devised by management to measure results.

THE IMPACT OF PERSONAL LEADERSHIP

I do not wish to present a picture of technological determinism. Important as task and technology are for channeling behavior, we find that some degrees of freedom are still left for the exercise of creative leadership. Let us assess the possibilities by getting down to cases.

In all my years of field research I have never encountered such an enthusiastic group of foremen and general foremen as my associates and I found working under division superintendent John Dyer and his superintendents. Dyer directed an organization of 700 men in one production unit of a very large company.

At the time Dyer took over his division, this and other plants at the same location had been run in a highly centralized fashion. Furthermore, the operation was in French Canada where the culture of family, church, and community seems to be somewhat more conducive to the acceptance of authority and to submissive behavior than it is in some other cultures. Nearly all the foremen and general foremen, as well as workers, were French Canadian, and they had not shown much inclination to challenge authority and express initiative in the past.

From the very beginning, John Dyer embarked upon a campaign to build up the initiative and freedom of action of his subordinates.

1. Dyer simplified the organization structure, removing the position of "supervisor" which had been between general foreman and superintendent.

2. General foremen were now authorized to sign requisitions for new employees and for new equipment (up to $1,000). Previously the superintendent had had to sign the slips.

3. Dyer broke down the barriers against free expression between subordinates and superiors by two means. First, he sought to informalize relations with his subordinates by promoting a series of evening social activities in which the men mixed freely and talked mainly about nonwork activities. He also circulated widely in the plant, dropping in on his foremen and general foremen frequently. On such occasions, he never told the men what to do or criticized their work. Sometimes there was simply an exchange of small talk. At other times the visit would lead to some discussion of work problems, but Dyer was careful to avoid giving answers and directions directly.

For management meetings he set a pattern of three-level discussion groups. Every month he led an extended discussion meeting with his superintendents and general foremen. Each of his two superintendents conducted monthly meetings with his general foremen and foremen. In time the general foremen themselves instituted monthly meetings with their foremen and workers.

The mechanics of the three-level meetings were not as important as the spirit within which they were conducted. Dyer made it known at the outset that the purpose of the meetings was to have a free exchange of opinions. If a general foreman disagreed with something that Dyer or one of the superintendents said, the man was to speak up and argue for his own point of view. Of course this instruction was not enough to change behavior. At first the foremen sat back to wait and see, but as they noticed that the superintendents could disagree with the big boss and have their contributions cordially received by him, the general foremen began to speak up themselves. They soon learned that there were no rewards for the man who simply agreed with the boss, whereas the man who took a different line—but made a good case for his position—received significant recognition. As the men got used to the new approach, the lid on communications really came off, and one could often observe vigorous expressions of disagreement between superior and subordinate in the division, either in pair situations or in group meetings.

The productivity of the division improved spectacularly under Dyer's leadership, and the development of the men was equally remarkable. We found them taking increased pride in their abilities and reaching out for new responsibilities.

Elsewhere I present this case in much greater detail.[1] I am offering

---

[1] William F. Whyte, *Men at Work*, Dorsey Press, Homewood, Ill., 1961.

here this brief summary mainly for what it tells us about the potential impact of managerial leadership upon conformity. In many organizations men seem to learn that conformity pays off in winning the favor of a boss. These foremen and general foremen learned that conformity to John Dyer's ideas would get them nowhere. In fact, too great a readiness to agree with the boss could be held against the man. When they learned that creative disagreement paid off, the foremen and general foremen went about expressing their opinions with greater freedom and frankness than I have ever seen in conversations between superiors and subordinates in any organization.

The case suggests that a skillful and imaginative executive can do a great deal to shift the balance of rewards and penalties so that it fosters independence and creativity rather than conformity.

TAKING INITIATIVE WITH THE BOSS

So far, we have been looking at leadership from the top down, as is customary. Recognizing that organizational position gives the superior more leverage in changing the behavior of the subordinate than the subordinate has in changing his boss, we have all tended to concentrate on the impact of the boss upon the organization. Nevertheless, let us now look up for a change. Suppose a man is working under an autocratic boss. Is it necessary, under these conditions, to surrender one's independence and become a yes-man in order to get ahead?

First, we should question the pragmatic effectiveness of yessing the boss—at least in many situations. Much as the boss may enjoy that crisp "yes" when he hears it, he may find that its repetition is not quite enough to build up his faith in his subordinates. The autocrat is not necessarily a stupid man. He may have just as good an eye for results as the next man. If he finds the personal relationship with the subordinate pleasant but the performance results poor, we may find the boss beginning to complain that his subordinates are weak individuals who don't have the initiative and the drive necessary to do the job.

Two qualifications to this statement should be noted. The flourishing of yes-men may depend in part upon the ease with which results can be measured. Where performance results are exceedingly difficult to measure, the man who can be consistently agreeable to the boss has the greatest opportunity for capitalizing on this talent. Whether the measurement of results will undo the agreeable but mediocre individual should also depend on the extent to which decisions and instructions from his boss will be reasonably adequate to cover the situations that a subordinate meets on the job. If they are, although the subordinate may appear to be getting the results, it is his superior who is really achieving them.

This discussion of yes-men has only scratched the surface of a complex subject. My purpose here is simply to raise questions about a commonly held assumption: that yessing the boss contributes to advancement in the business organization. I have sought to point out that agreement pays off in some situations more than in others and that, in any case, it is hardly safe for the ambitious executive to assume that conformity, per se, will help him to get ahead.

Suppose our man serving under an autocratic boss wishes to increase substantially his own freedom of action—and still remain within the organization. Can he do anything about it?

The case of Wes Walsh suggests that he can. Walsh was superintendent of a plant of about the same size as John Dyer's. He came in under a works manager widely known in the company for his type of autocratic control. Furthermore, the offices of the two men were within a hundred feet of each other, so that although the boss was also responsible for other plants in the area, he could keep a close watch over Walsh. Nevertheless, Walsh was able to manage his plant very much according to his own notions, with little interference from above. How did he do it?

The previous superintendent had been constantly at swords' points with the works manager. He advised Walsh to keep away from the manager's office. "The less you see of that son of a bitch, the better you'll get along." Though Walsh and his predecessor were good friends, Walsh decided to disregard the advice. If it hadn't worked for his predecessor, why should it work for him? Instead, Walsh saw to it that he had frequent contacts with the boss—and contacts that were initiated primarily by Walsh himself. He would drop in, with apparent casualness, to report progress or to seek the works manager's approval on some minor matter, carefully selected so that the boss could hardly veto it. Walsh was getting his boss used to saying yes to him!

Major matters required longer interaction between the men, carefully prepared and staged. Consider the problems of the materials-reprocessing unit.

With increasing volume of production going through the plant, it had become apparent to Walsh—as indeed it had to his predecessor—that this unit was inadequate for current requirements. It was too slow in operation and too limited in capacity. This condition seriously hampered production and created a storage problem in the plant. Materials awaiting reprocessing were strewn about at one end of the operating area.

Walsh's first step was to propose to the boss that he pick a time when he could spend a couple of hours with Walsh in the plant, so that they could look over some of the problems the plant was facing. The manager set the time, and the two men spent the hours together on an inspection tour. To some extent the physical conditions the works manager saw spoke for themselves, but Walsh also supplemented these visual clues with an account of the way in which the inadequacy of the materials-reprocessing unit hampered his operations. The boss had to agree that the condition was undesirable. Eventually he asked, "What do you propose?"

Walsh was ready with a carefully worked-out proposal for the purchase of a new type of reprocessing unit at a cost of $150,000. After a brief discussion of the impact of a new machine on costs and production, the works manager authorized the purchase. It is noteworthy that essentially the same proposal had been made more than once to the works manager by Walsh's predecessor. Made no doubt in a different form and fitting into a different context of interpersonal relationships, the good idea had received simply a flat rejection.

So effectively did Wes Walsh handle his superior that he won a large measure of freedom from a man known throughout the works as an autocrat. And the works manager was more than happy with the relationship. In fact, several years later, after his own retirement, he was boasting to others about how he had discovered and developed Wes Walsh!

Walsh adds two qualifying comments to the story of his success. He points out that the works manager was approaching retirement, that he lacked firsthand experience with the plant managed by Walsh, and that he was preoccupied with pressing problems in another plant. "If he had been ten years younger, he would have found the time and the energy to get to know my plant inside out, and then he would have given me a much harder time." We should add, nevertheless, that the same conditions had prevailed for Walsh's immediate predecessor, and that he had been completely unable to gain any freedom of action.

Walsh suggests these rules for approaching a big decision with an autocratic boss:

1. Prepare the ground carefully; don't just spring it on the boss.

2. Don't present the problem and the proposed solution at the same time.

3. Present the problem in stages and in such a way that no solution will be immediately apparent to the boss. This will help to assure you that he does not commit himself before you have had a chance to make your full case. Once an executive of this type has committed himself, it is almost impossible to get him to reverse his decision. If you can bring him through all phases of the problem with the solution still unclear in his mind, then your chances of getting your solution accepted are greatly improved.

It is not my purpose to suggest that Wes Walsh has discovered *the* way to deal with an autocratic boss. That would be a gross oversimplification. I cite his story only in order to show that a skillful and imaginative executive can win himself considerable freedom of action from bosses whom many would consider intolerable autocrats.

CONCLUSION

The cases of Wes Walsh and John Dyer suggest to me that an executive can, at least in some situations, build an atmosphere of creativity for his subordinates and also win freedom to express his own individuality. The introductory discussion has also implied that task, technology, and organization structure may greatly limit or increase possibilities of freedom of action. However, we should note also that these forces are themselves subject to the decisions of men—as we have seen in the experience of John Dyer in effecting a change in organization structure.

A creative leader will not limit his efforts in human relations to the immediate face-to-face contacts. He will consider task, technology, and organization structure from the standpoint of their effect upon human beings as well as upon technical efficiency, and he will find new ways to integrate these forces with personal leadership.

The creative leader will recognize the problem of adjustment between the individual and the organization. However, he will not take the advice of William H. Whyte, Jr., and simply fight the organization. He will regard the organization as something to be studied and understood just as technology, cost-control procedures, and other aspects of business may be studied and understood. He will then seek to reshape the organization so that it functions more effectively to serve human as well as material ends.

The executive who can increase the areas of creativity for himself and his subordinates is indeed a skillful leader, but if these skills are to be understood and taught to others, we must not consider them simply as attributes of a unique personality. This type of thinking leads to a dead end in leadership studies.

Taking the usual personality approach, what are we to say to other executives who wish to achieve the results won by Dyer and Walsh? Go thou and be like John Dyer? In fact, no one is just like Dyer, and any effort to imitate his particular combination of personality traits is bound to fail. Basically, people have to be themselves; there is nobody else they can be. If we examine instead the *actions* and human *interactions* of such men, we shall be able to lay out a systematic pattern of behavior that other men may follow even though their personalities seem to be quite different from those of Dyer and Walsh.

This is not the place to present such a systematic statement, but I can at least point out some of the types of observations that need to be made and analyzed.

Note that Dyer, compared with his predecessor, greatly increased the frequency of the general superintendent's interactions with lower-level management people. Since he avoided punitive measures in these pair interactions, the increased frequency served to build positive sentiments to the big boss and also to stimulate subordinates to express themselves to him.

The interlocking network of three-level meetings involves an organization of interactions that can be quite specifically described. We can also note that when, in such a meeting, a subordinate makes a suggestion or disagrees with the big boss, he is encouraged to extend the duration of his interactions in the meeting (to talk further on the topic). By way of contrast, a stated agreement with the big boss does not elicit any invitation to continue talking. Instead, the boss initiates interaction with someone else on the same topic or goes on to raise another topic with the group as a whole.

In comparison with his predecessor, we note that Walsh greatly increased his interactions with his boss—by himself initiating as high a proportion of them as possible. He also sought to structure these interactions into a pattern of assent: presenting simple proposals that seemed to require yes answers.

Such statements as these oversimplify complex problems. They are designed only to illustrate that it is possible to observe and describe man-boss relations in an objective manner. If that is true, then we can substitute analysis of interaction patterns for the futile search for the "qualities of leadership."

A NOTE

As Whyte has stated, there is no immutable relationship between the size of an organization and the welfare of the individual or the opportunity for development it provides him. Jibes at social scientists who seek to study the relations between organizational mechanisms and human behavior for their interest in "manipulation" are hardly appropriate in an age where large institutions predominate.

It would be wasteful to review all of Professor Whyte's ideas; they are presented with clarity. One point we would emphasize is an example of the intimate relationship between structure and behavior. Whyte mentions controls. Recently at Columbia we had the privilege of hearing from Thomas Watson, chairman of the IBM Corporation. Watson observed that the corporation's sales personnel had always seemed to demonstrate somewhat more initiative, more risk-taking ability, even more ambition to get ahead than had comparable executives in some other areas of the business. On investigation, their drive was shown to be a product not of the type of person attracted to these jobs but rather of the availability of a clear measure of success: sales volume. In other parts of the business, managers were less likely to take chances with nonconformity because their contribution might never be identified and rewarded. On the other hand, failure could be very costly. Thus, the balance between potential rewards and punishments, very much within the control of top management, can explain differences in individual performance.

chapter 17

The organization man: how real a problem? *

Recently we have witnessed a new variation on the old theme that business destroys (or at least eats away) the souls of those who come within its grasp. The eating-away process used to refer to ethics and morality. Caught up in the profit-making system, men who otherwise might dedicate themselves to a life of unselfish service sought instead a far tinnier Holy Grail—the almighty dollar. Although as generalizations about an entire system these condemnations embodied exaggerations, they had the virtue of sensitizing the community to excesses. A growing sense of business responsibility and protection against willful discharge and sweatshop servitude may to some extent be due to their harsh repetition. If this is true, then there may be a virtue in what is otherwise a somewhat puzzling new accusation: Life in the business organization induces excessive conformity and dependence.[1]

---

* This material was presented at the conference and later published in Eliot D. Chapple and Leonard R. Sayles, *The Measure of Management*, The Macmillan Company, New York, 1961. Copyright by The Macmillan Company, 1961.

[1] Two of the most extensive nonfiction works representing this new critique of business are: William H. Whyte, Jr., *The Organization Man*, Simon and Schuster, Inc., New York, 1956; and (with a very different point of view) Chris Argyris, *Personality and Organization*, Harper & Row, Publishers, Incorporated, New York, 1957. A recent fictionalized account of the debilitations induced by the large corporation is Alan Harrington's *Life in the Crystal Palace*, Alfred A. Knopf, Inc., New York, 1959.

The critics do not mean that people caught up in the soulless web of the corporation are converted into money-grubbing robots or ever-fearful wage slaves. They say, rather, that contemporary organizations are a threat to the psyche. Employees and managers in our large companies lose their sense of independence, their pluck, and their daring. Instead of devoting themselves to highly individualistic programs of self-improvement (money-grubbing?), they become dedicated to the seductive goals of being accepted and even being liked by boss and colleague. These are the organization men.

The highly negative fear of losing acceptance becomes the dominating motive, to replace the more positive goal of conquering new frontiers. The critics argue that conforming to the group and kowtowing to the boss absorb all the energies which might be more healthily devoted to constructive development of personality and the corporate and community balance sheet. The result must be slow but sure destruction of national character.

Perhaps the generous reception given to the organization-man image is a hallmark of our steady progress in humanizing the conditions of work and the position of the subordinate. Rather than the callous, over-demanding boss who gets what he wants regardless of the human cost, we are apparently now concerned with his diametric opposite—the group thinker who is more concerned with social cohesion than he is with profit. Surely we have now come around the full circle. Less than two decades ago Elton Mayo's fear about the lack of administrators who could banish the sense of individual isolation (or "anomie," the concept he drew from Durkheim) was the accepted tenet of faith.

As more adherents join a bandwagon that has the additional lure of playing a quasipsychiatric theme, one is reminded of the extremes of "progressive" education and child rearing. Not long ago, the home and the school were the villains. Both at the hearth and at the blackboard our young were being repressed, their individualism squashed long before it could flower. The reasoning was much the same—humans flourish best in an unfettered, unrestricted, free-to-do-as-they-please environment. Fixity of structure, it was insisted, must produce rigidity of mind. The extremists felt, as does the organization-is-an-inhibitor school of thought, that discipline and controls, externally imposed goals, hurt the individual who both desired and needed complete freedom.

Parenthetically, we might ask why the concept of an "organization man" has had such wide and immediate appeal. Is it not the perfect self-rationalization for those individuals whose success has not measured up to their ambitions? They are reassured by the belief that group thinking and conformity have so won over the decision makers in our large corporations that the individual who stands out from the crowd cannot get ahead. Some who use this ready-made excuse confuse the lip service given by companies to presently popular clichés like "teamwork" and "participation" with an actual description of what management expects. Platitudinous statements concerning objectives, values, or goals may bear little resemblance to the types of activities in which a company engages. The organization, as we shall be observing, both needs and rewards distinctive and unique personality characteristics such as high energy, initiative, and the ability to tolerate unfriendly responses. They may talk about a good "team man," but the uncommon men are the ones who will get ahead and eventually reach the top-level positions.

OPPOSITE FINDINGS FROM RESEARCH

Students of man cannot help but be amused by this whole surprising trend in the critique of business. There are no studies that show man in some Eden-like status of complete independence. In the most primitive state and in all the records of history, man has sought and flourished in tribes and clans, communities, and associations. If half a dozen people are placed in a room with a common task, we can predict they will quickly evolve common routines of behavior and even a self-imposed organizational structure. The latter will include leadership to initiate instructions, and the group will penalize deviations from approved standards of behavior. Conformity will be expected, and dependence will be readily forthcoming. The street-corner gang, like the office clique, makes such excessive demands for conformity in thought and action with an impunity that makes the routines of the organization and the demands of its authority pale by comparison.

Man apparently neither wants nor has experienced this postulated state of complete autonomy. People have always demanded structure in their lives. With few exceptions, men depend on human relationships, some fixity of structure, routine, and habit to survive psychologically. Although we do not like to admit it, most of us flee from a vacuumlike absence of structured relationships. Students of business organization know well that one of management's basic problems is to find enough people with characteristics of leadership who will take initiative and who can operate in a relatively unstructured situation. The demand of subordinates for situations in which they can be dependent, not the supply of overbearing authority, is frequently the problem. Companies seeking to make decentralization operative discover, to their sorrow, that unwillingness to accept responsibility or to take initiative, and the desire to have each decision sanctified by the boss's OK are ever-present blocks to successful delegation.

What about the emotional needs of the man on the work level? Is it not true that extremes of the division of labor and autocratic, dominating supervisors rob the individual of any real sense of accomplishment and satisfaction in his job?

Put in these terms, this concern might also be shown to be misplaced. Many workers voluntarily choose the simplest, most routine, most subdivided task. While job enlargement must appeal to some, for many it is a threat to the more idyllic assurance of untroubled working hours, free for daydreaming, social chatter, and strategic planning to "beat the rate." Employees certainly do not always seek additional responsibility and decreased dependence.

THE NATURE OF ORGANIZATION

Contemporary fiction, sermons, and social science have become enamoured of their moans over the fate of the individual in the large organization. Unfortunately, the eagerness with which the term "organization man" has been adopted has resulted in substantial confusion, a good portion of which stems from its original promulgation. The essence of organization, of organizational behavior, involves learning to follow routine procedures. Of necessity the organization must be a predictable system of human relationships, where rhythm and repetition are the vital components. This may come as a rude shock to those who think of managers as constantly improvising new activities. Chester Barnard once commented candidly that during a year as president of the New Jersey Bell Telephone Company he had to make only *one* decision that was, in fact, a real choice between alternatives. The preponderant elements of organizational behavior consist of matters such as Joe's knowing that he must check Bill's activities two or three times a week, must be available when Al gets into trouble, and must sit with his boss at least an hour a day to work through plans for the following day. The combination of work-flow imperatives and personality needs provide the raw material for these predictable and rhythmical patterns of interaction.

It must be remembered that in speaking of an organization we imply some degree of permanence—the need for predictable repetition, self-maintenance, assured continuity, and regulated activity. Only when the regular business of an organization is functioning properly—following the *routines* of acquisition, processing, and distribution (of ideas, materials, or paper)—can individuals apply, or are they likely to be permitted to apply, their rational, creative talents to the challenge of new, unsolved problems. Imagination, innovation, and intellectual vigor cannot prosper where individual energies are fully utilized in handling recurring crises.

In this regard, the president of the Brookings Institution recently observed:

If administrators are asked to nominate the aspects of the task that are most time-consuming and frustrating to the exercise of their responsibilities, they will agree that they are preoccupied with distractions; with inconsequential little things that push themselves ahead of important issues; with the tyranny of the telephone; with the relentless flitting from one issue to another; with the ceaseless procession of interviews and ceremonials; with the pressure of circumstance and deadlines; and with the absence of time to collect one's wits, much less to think or reflect. Only a superb or a hard-boiled administrator can cut through this daily morass to concentrate on the important responsibilities that he cannot shirk.[2]

Although Barnard's statement may well be something of an exaggeration, among the most crucial problems of any organization are those concerned with the development of predictable routines. Frayed tempers, suppressed and not so suppressed, hostility, and individual frustration resulting from ineffective organization destroy individual competence.

In other fields in which organization plays a part we are not so shocked by this. The most dramatic and best known is sport. Baseball and football teams are the most common examples of organizations

[2] Robert D. Calkins, "The Decision Process in Administration," *Business Horizons*, vol. 2, no. 3, p. 20, Fall, 1952.

where the interrelation of the work routines (the plays) is dependent upon the careful adjustment of players to one another and to the coaches. Here complicated plays and split-second coordination cannot be executed unless the organization is made up of individuals well adjusted to one another. The job of the coach is to see that this is accomplished, to select a series of plays best fitted to the capacities of his materials, and to fit together players who can supplement each other's abilities. To develop a smooth-working organization, he must handle personalities so skillfully that good teamwork becomes almost second nature. As a result, the experts and the fans discuss learnedly whether coach A is getting the most out of his material, whether catcher B can handle his pitchers, whether star C is wrecking the morale of the team.

Business organizations are like teams, but vastly more complicated. The same factors of plays and personalities combine to make an organization, and the adjustment that goes on from day to day determines whether the company is to have effective coordination or will constantly suffer from personnel dissatisfaction, labor disputes, and inefficiency.[3]

Does this necessity create "organization men"? Members of outstanding instrumental groups like the Budapest String Quartet have developed almost perfect coordination; they can count on each other for completely predictable behavior. It is doubtful that this coordination has destroyed their individuality. Off the job, in the full development of their personalities and interests, they live very different lives. Great athletic teams have consisted of people who had little liking for one another—e.g., "Tinker to Evers to Chance"—amply demonstrating their uncongeniality in their personal lives. Nevertheless, they learned the skills and routines essential for the successful conduct of their organizational affairs.

One would hazard a guess that a great deal of the excitement about conformity is due to the *absence* of knowledge concerning what is required for effective organizational activity, like the primitive tribe that does not understand the movements of the heavenly bodies and the occurrence of thunderstorms. Not knowing how to assess Jones's contribution to effective management, we evolve irrational fetishes and

---

[3] We hope the reader will not think we are indulging in the old stereotype of the company president in exhorting his coworkers, "We're all on the same team, boys." We are not talking about "togetherness," but the development and synchronization of a complex set of plays (organization) by which the company operates.

taboos. The striped tie, the ivy-league suit, the sheepskin, the appropriate tone of voice, automobile, wife, and home location, even the testing programs designed to exclude all but the "safe" pedestrian types: these are all manifestations of imperfect knowledge about how to evaluate an executive or a new employee. They are not the inevitable products of life in a large organization.

As we develop more understanding about methods of improving the mastery of organizational behavior, we can believe that the nonsensical elements will disappear just as rain dances have fallen into disrepute in most civilized locations. Fitting personalities together to evolve coordination and sound structure does not require fixed patterns of thought and of family and community life.

We must be careful to urge businessmen to deal with real problem areas, not those that may be the easiest to sell during a period when terms like *conformity* are so popular. The human relations problems of business will not be solved by extreme, sweeping assertions and accusations, any more than the field of mental health will be improved by arguments that neuroses are enveloping us all. It has always been good sport to beat at our sources of institutional power, including business, and one of the strengths of Western democracy has been this permissive climate. But we must not confuse sermons with science. We readily concede that there are problems of large scale in contemporary life. Mass communications, for example, in our type of society raise serious questions concerning opportunities for individual expression, privilege in democracy that we rightfully cherish. Further, living with authority, of course, has never been easy. Philosophers undoubtedly will continue to struggle with one of the persistent problems of life: freedom versus authority. The balance is always a tenuous one. Life in the presence of other human beings involves cooperative endeavors and government, and consequently necessitates authority. We must always live with an uneasy balance between the inevitable personal restrictions and our ambivalent needs for both dependence and freedom. The problem neither began nor will it end with the corporation.

THE MODERN MANAGER VERSUS
THE BUSINESS BUCCANEER

As an alternative to this straw man, the organization man, the old-style business buccaneer is having a renaissance. In the current swing to idolize the swashbuckler, even the robber baron has had a resurrection. After all, weren't these the true believers—the noncomformists who allowed neither codes nor public disapproval nor built-in inhibition to stand in the way of their single-minded objectives? By contrast, the contemporary manager, concerned with public and industrial relations and with an organizational structure to maximize human effectiveness, at best casts only a faint shadow. Or so the critics would have us believe.

It is strange indeed that the contemporary manager is now being maligned for what is his greatest challenge and potential accomplishment. The maintenance of effective human relationships in large-scale organizations is one of the marvels of our age. The skills of administration required to direct and control tens of thousands of people with differing backgrounds and interests, in order to produce coordinated effort directed toward predetermined objectives, tower above the achievements of the business buccaneers of an earlier age. They dealt with a few, simple variables primarily in the market place. Their apparent bravery and daring were more a product of the simplicity of their problem than of extraordinary skills or brute native courage. The diverse and complex responsibilities of the modern business offer a challenge many times more exciting to human abilities than an uncomplicated "inner-directed" objective of maximum personal profits.

Appendix

The subject of this symposium is one that has encouraged more speculation than research. It is just as tempting to damn the large organization as it is to find reasons for praising its contributions. Within the social sciences themselves there are sharp disagreements, and frequently discussions of the human problems of industry produce more heat than light. Management techniques to motivate the individual have had many advocates; yet few, if any, of the techniques have been validated. The sharply opposed generalizations that follow are designed to illustrate some of the problems and existing conflicts of opinion that need to be resolved if progress is to be made in research and in greater understanding of the role of the individual in the contemporary large organization.

I. WHAT DOES MANAGEMENT EXPECT FROM THE INDIVIDUAL EMPLOYEE?

What type of person does management seek?
Is conformity a problem?

1. (*a*) Sustained health and the potentiality for growth in a company demands that the organization attract, develop, and encourage the determined individualist who will allow neither red tape nor sentiment to stand in the way of accomplishment.

    (*b*) Although we may want to idealize individualism, in fact, organizational effectiveness depends upon the development of smoothly operating routines and thus upon the activities of people who have developed collaborative and integrative skills. There may be a few jobs in which the "lone wolf" can make an outstanding contribution (e.g., some research work), but they are in the minority.

185

The *team* player, not the rugged individualist, is the person most frequently needed.

2. (*a*) Contemporary organizations do not stimulate present-day executives to develop the same pluck and determination that was characteristic of an earlier generation of entrepreneurs and businessmen —highly individualistic risk taking, perseverance, and dedication. (*b*) The successful manager today has just as much challenge, and is worthy of just as much praise for his success in administering large, complex business institutions, as the promoter or innovator of yesterday. In fact these skills of management are perhaps more difficult and more important than the simpler attributes of risk taking and trading astuteness that were characteristic of earlier entrepreneurs.

3. (*a*) There is no firm evidence that the basic nature of people has changed over a period of time in our nation or elsewhere. In each age, the historian, the student of human affairs, and the writer have thought they have observed a softening in moral fiber and ambition, perhaps a growing unfavorable balance between leaders and followers in the population. The proportion today of dominant, initiating, highly motivated people is probably as great as it was earlier in our country's history. (*b*) A number of social scientists have documented the growing conformity in our culture: the interest in consumption rather than production, in popularity rather than in high performance. This trend, resulting from forces both inside and outside the company, is a new and challenging problem with which the organization must deal.

How important should the job be in the life of the employee?

1. (*a*) The goal of the organization should be to obtain maximum performance from the individual; to challenge and utilize as much of the inherent capacity of its members as possible. To attain these goals the organization should provide a milieu in which the individual's basic satisfactions can be realized. (*b*) It is unrealistic and it may be politically inappropriate to hope that the individual will satisfy most of his needs at his place of work. Our pluralistic society offers a man many opportunities to express his personality, and except in a few unusual, top-level jobs, one

should not expect to find the organization completely satisfying to all its members.

II. THE IMPACT OF THE LARGE ORGANIZATION ON INDIVIDUALS: EVALUATING THE EVIDENCE

Is most work inhibiting and restrictive in large organizations?

1. (*a*) There is no reason to believe that a large organization will be more or less confining than a small organization. Human beings spend their lifetimes developing mechanisms of adjustment to the presence and activity of other people, some of whom have power and control over them. A small company (or family!) headed by a tyrant can be as stifling to initiative as the more regimented larger organization; and of course the small, family-owned business frequently provides little opportunity for the ambitious "outsider" to get ahead.

   (*b*) Large organizations, whether public or private, tend to become rigid and less receptive to the spontaneous activity and ideas of their members. Inevitably they are more confining, breed dependency, inhibit the mature development of the personality, and as a result succeed in tapping less of the individual's potential than do smaller organizations.

2. (*a*) Large organizations have pioneered in the establishment of internal systems of due process and personnel management that protect the individual from arbitrary supervision and capricious decisions affecting his status, income, and working conditions. The sense of equity and security these systems encourage is a necessary base or prerequisite for the individual who is going to excel and, in extending himself, assume risks. In fact, just because of its size and resulting spaciousness, the larger organization is more likely to contain a niche for the unusual, nonconformist employee.

   (*b*) The large organization, because of its massiveness, fixed policies, and many-leveled hierarchy, encourages dependency and thus inevitably conformity and its by-product, mediocrity.

3. (*a*) Individuals have the obligation to *accommodate* themselves to the requirements of other people; in fact this accommodation is one

of the best criteria of maturity. The organization, by requiring such compromises, is not stifling the individual, but is providing an environment consistent with nearly every other aspect of human endeavor: the family, the church, political parties, and other community groups. Furthermore, individuals can retain their values and autonomy while learning to live within a somewhat confining environment.

(b) The requirements for relatively fixed patterns of behavior, conformity to channels and rules, and the need to *adjust* one's conduct to the demands of a large, authoritarian organization necessarily conflict with the expression of a mature personality. Relatively narrow, precisely defined jobs and bureaucratic "trappings" are more consistent with immature, dependent personalities than with adult needs.

4. (a) The individual's personality is relatively fixed by the time he enters the company. His ability and willingness to contribute his ideas and energy are largely products of his personality. The able, initiating, determined employee finds a way to express himself, even when he endures organizational handicaps; the excessively timid, compliant individual will always find excuses for failing to contribute, no matter what organizational structure he functions in or how few or how many people surround him.

(b) By their very nature, large, complex organizations with specific policies, fixed channels, and many levels handicap the individual in expressing his personality and in so doing minimize the total contribution they receive from their members.

5. (a) Large organizations can afford to allow the individual some leeway, to take risks, to make "long shots," to follow risky paths of exploration where the chances of immediate payoff are small but the potentials are great. These are the companies that pioneer in the adoption of new ideas, new technologies, and methods which represent the expression of individual initiative and risk taking.

(b) The evidence suggests that the large company evolves an atmosphere of caution, discouraging to the individual who wants to initiate and innovate. As one sociologist so aptly said, "Living dangerously was never very attractive to very many, but the peril of prosperity (one might substitute the term *organization success*) is that it permits so many to avoid risk and still prosper."

Do organizations become more rigid and bureaucratic with age?

1. (*a*) Organizations tend to *change* over periods of time; organizations contain the seeds of their own reform and are, at different times, more and less rigid. One of the sources of change is the pattern of responses people will make to *excessive* rigidity—responses emerging out of the personality's need for variety and change, for challenge and excitement. Another source of change is the pressure that will be generated outside the company by failures to meet the expectations of consumers, stockholders, and other interest groups. While there may be inevitable lags, the company that fails to adapt to changing times eventually pays a heavy penalty, which in turn becomes the stimulus that sets off change.

   (*b*) Organizations tend to stabilize and to become rigid; they therefore not only block the expression of individuality and creativity but they tend to do so increasingly over time, until they become bureaucratic and static. This tendency is reinforced by their penchant for being selective in recruitment and promotion: for selecting personality types that will not "rock the boat."

2. (*a*) Organizations have many built-in mechanisms, often not noted by critics, through which the individual can express the diverse facets of his personality. There are always informal or extralegal procedures by which groups of colleagues and associates modify the formal rules and procedures to evolve a work environment suitable to their own needs. While this "shadow" organization does not appear on the formal charts, it is of major significance in explaining how individuals tailor their jobs to fit their needs.

   (*b*) *Bureaucracy*, the best term to characterize large organizations, means relatively fixed job descriptions, which assume that the individual will not express his own personality but will fit into a predetermined mold. He will be rewarded and advanced according to how well he succeeds in suppressing his own reactions and acts the role of the bureaucrat or organization man. Impersonality, mechanization, self-control, and desire to avoid calling attention to oneself by always making the safe decision are attributes which best characterize this system.

III. MECHANISMS FOR INCREASING INDIVIDUAL INITIATIVE AND PRODUCTIVITY IN THE LARGE ORGANIZATION

What will be the long-run effect of automation and improvements in the "management sciences"?

1. (a) Gradually improved organization controls and methods of assessing individual and department performance will encourage greater emphasis on management by results. Clique membership, favoritism, and "politicking" will become less important in affecting decision making, and individual managers will be motivated to gain recognition and advancement by effective performance.

(b) Improvements in the management sciences are likely to accent the hierarchical nature of the organization. Closer supervision can be exercised by top management and less leeway provided for decision making and initiative at lower levels of the organization.

2. (a) The trend in large organizations is toward more routine jobs and the concentration of creativity and initiative in the hands of a small group of staff experts and top managers.

(b) Automation and better organization design serve to eliminate or minimize the importance of routine, undemanding jobs. The trend is clearly toward using more of the individual's special talents, leaving to systems and equipment the mechanical, routinizable operations.

Can job enlargement and other techniques to make work more interesting be useful?

1. (a) As our growing economy has provided greater satisfaction of economic or basic physical needs, the relative importance of psychological needs has increased. Most jobs are so designed that they fail to motivate initiative and effort because they provide no intrinsic psychological satisfaction. The opportunity to earn these satisfactions would be the best type of incentive for the individual.

(b) It is unrealistic to try to return to a simpler technology. Many employees voluntarily select the simpler, less responsible jobs. We have tended to glorify the past—when work hours were long and exhausting. Today, even on routine jobs, the employee usually has the opportunity to develop a satisfying social life.

What is the probable impact of the decentralization movement?

1. (*a*) Decentralization gives the large firm the advantage of small size and enhances the motivational appeals to the individual manager.

(*b*) The advantages of decentralization have been exaggerated. Trends in technology, computer development, and the management sciences point clearly in the direction of more centralized structures. Furthermore, it is unrealistic to ignore the fact that we are living in an age of large organizations which are more likely to increase in size than to get smaller.

Can improved promotional opportunities and merit awards motivate the individual?

1. (*a*) As long as an organization continues to grow and provide advancement opportunities for its members—greater income and higher status—motivated managers will struggle to attain clearly announced organizational goals and to win a greater share of the available rewards for themselves. In so doing they will "give their all."

(*b*) Gradually the incentive to advance oneself is being blunted so that promotional opportunities do not have the same motivating force they had a generation ago. Individuals prefer security, family satisfactions, and less rather than more responsibility. Tax laws and our leisure-oriented society are fast eroding the individual's desire to get ahead by maximum performance.

2. (*a*) There is still a vast untapped reservoir of techniques to reward the outstanding individual contributor.

(*b*) In many organizations the potential rewards for innovating and taking responsible, decisive action are small, while the penalties are very great for "sticking your neck out" (particularly when your decision turns out not to have been the correct one).

3. (*a*) Even the Russians have learned the value of differential payment plans, whereby the highly skilled and proficient earn substantially more than those whose performance is not so valuable.

The heyday of union pressures for decreased differentials and a flat rate for the job has passed, and certainly in non-blue-collar work there must always be the extended "carrot"—the possibility of very substantial additional earnings with increased job skill and responsibility.

(b) There is little to encourage management about its potential ability to reward and thus motivate individual performance. Most measurement devices are not valid (e.g., "merit rating"), and most productivity is a result of group effort.

Does the increasing of fringe benefits aid or hinder efforts to motivate the individual?

1. (a) Large companies, by pioneering in the development of greater employee security, stability of employment, equitable and adequate wage plans, through developments in personnel management such as pension programs, and protections against arbitrary layoffs and discharge, have served to free the individual from haunting economic insecurities. These fears restrain a man from contributing his maximum energies. Guarantees of due process for the individual within the organization (e.g., grievance procedures) provide the same stimulating environment for the individual that a democratic political life provides for the nation as a whole; the guarantees are like the citizens' constitution.

(b) The growth of fringe benefits reinforces the declining interest of employees in their jobs. Except for doing a minimum job to guarantee tenure, employees have their interests directed toward longer vacations, retirement, and other time off the job (or time-and-a-half pay for time on the job).

How important are improvements in supervisory techniques and the use of group methods?

1. (a) The qualities of democratic supervision, or participative management as it is sometimes called, serve to develop subordinates and bring forth more subordinate initiative and higher motivation than do the more autocratic, traditional techniques of management.

(*b*) The evidence is mounting that neither do subordinates expect more participation in management nor does the organization flourish when there is an overemphasis on democratic supervision, particularly when this is at the expense of adequate controls.

2. (*a*) An undue emphasis in recent years has been placed on the qualities of good supervision. Poor performance and inefficiency is more likely to be caused by poor organization design (e.g., the manner in which jobs are grouped together in departments, the chains of command, and the relationship of staff to line groups) than by inadequate administrative skill. For example, the hoped-for repealing of "Parkinson's Law" promises to free more initiative than almost any other endeavor on the part of management. Many employees are stifled by the sheer weight of numbers, the proliferation of people—staff, service, and line—to complete jobs that were once done by a much smaller number. When management learns how to appraise work loads correctly for nonrepetitive, salaried, and executive positions, this better distribution will solve many of the problems of obtaining maximum contributions from the individual.

(*b*) Lack of good leadership in the organization is a primary cause of low individual productivity. Given better managers, we should expect higher performance.

3. (*a*) It is not surprising that large business has turned to group decision involving the contributions of staff expert research and management committees. Americans have always shied away from dogmatic assertions and the belief in a discoverable best or only way. As a people, they have always been more pragmatic than theoretical, interested in exploring and testing many alternatives, and dubious about their own convictions and the correctness of their first impulses. In addition, as companies have grown larger and more complex, the decisions that must be made have grown proportionately, and one man frequently cannot have all the necessary information and/or is reluctant to make major commitments without the counsel of others. The argument can also be made that it is easy to overemphasize the importance of decision making. Chester Barnard once commented that as president of New Jersey Bell he made only one or two real decisions a year. Finally, broadening the number of people consulted on, or contributing to, deci-

sion making helps to train and develop subordinates for more responsible decisions.

(b) One of the most deleterious aspects of large organizations is the camouflage provided by such mechanisms as committees for those who want to avoid *individual responsibility*. By hiding in the group, the executive does not have to develop, or ever learn to develop, those qualities of risk taking and decisiveness so essential to the successful conduct of top-executive jobs.

What is the appropriate place of personality testing?

1. (a) Personality tests help to place people in jobs which will enable them to utilize their talents. As long as someone has to make selection decisions, particularly for managerial positions, the element of personality is going to play an important part in that decision. There is no longer much question that personality characteristics are a vital part of successful management. Tests seek merely to systematize the evaluation of that component. By excluding people who cannot work effectively in an organization, testing increases the likelihood that other members will have the opportunity to express their abilities more fully. Personality conflicts are not conducive to creative thinking.

(b) No matter how justified, personality testing inevitably has a deleterious effect on initiative and creativity in the organization. At some point in such programs those responsible for setting the criteria for selection decide that there is an easy solution to the problems of effective management—excluding the unusual, the potentially difficult, in fact the strong personality. A kind of lowest common denominator begins to emerge as the ideal company type, usually the safe, easily managed, uncreative person.

From one point of view such a list as the one above can be discouraging; there are so many contradictions and loopholes, so many instances where an argument on one side of a question can be met with an equally convincing argument that leads to a diametrically opposed conclusion. It is true that the evidence accumulated to date within business itself and by social scientists is contradictory and confusing and frequently fails to give direction to managements that are seeking actively to improve their utilization of the individual.

Many of us who have been concerned with the development of this symposium believe the answer lies in the direction of more careful research, directed specifically toward the issues suggested here, and in an avoidance of easy slogans and pat solutions.

Index